the
good
life

the
good
life

30 steps to perfecting the art of living

MARK VERNON

For UK order enquiries: please contact Bookpoint Ltd, 130 Milton Park, Abingdon, Oxon OX14 4SB. Telephone: +44 (0) 1235 827720. Fax: +44 (0) 1235 400454. Lines are open 09.00–17.00, Monday to Saturday, with a 24-hour message answering service. Details about our titles and how to order are available at www.teachyourself.com

British Library Cataloguing in Publication Data: a catalogue record for this title is available from the British Library.

Library of Congress Catalog Card Number: on file.

First published in UK 2010 by Hodder Education, part of Hachette UK, 338 Euston Road, London NW1 3BH.

Typeset by Servis Filmsetting Ltd, Stockport, Cheshire.
Printed in Great Britain for Hodder Education, an Hachette UK Company, 338 Euston Road, London NW1 3BH, by CPI Cox & Wyman, Reading, Berkshire RG1 8EX.

The publisher has used its best endeavours to ensure that the URLs for external websites referred to in this book are correct and active at the time of going to press. However, the publisher and the author have no responsibility for the websites and can make no guarantee that a site will remain live or that the content will remain relevant, decent or appropriate.

Hachette UK's policy is to use papers that are natural, renewable and recyclable products and made from wood grown in sustainable forests. The logging and manufacturing processes are expected to conform to the environmental regulations of the country of origin.

Impression number 10 9 8 7 6 5 4 3 2 1
Year 2014 2013 2012 2011 2010

Contents

Introduction

Advice on how to live is hardly in short supply these days. And that fact, in itself, might give us pause for thought. Why, we may wonder, is it such a growth industry? It's 150 years since the Scottish writer Samuel Smiles published the first avowed self-help book (and the first to carry the title *Self-Help*). Think of all the advice that's appeared since, all that good sense! So how come we've still not worked it out?

Many of the self-help books published these days draw on new insights from psychology. Or at least, they are *claimed* as new insights. What psychologists do, more or less, is assemble groups of people – often students, since they are cheap to hire and ready to hand – and ask them how they feel about, say, keeping resolutions or being liked. The psychologists then process the responses, with statistics, and publish the means and averages. *Voilà!* New insights.

Now, I don't want to offend any students, but I'm not so sure about this whole process. The science certainly produces empirically based results. And you want that if you're having heart surgery. But what about the more subtle, less mechanical questions of living? If you, an individual, apply those means and averages to your life, is it surprising that the benefits can seem a bit mean and average? I notice it when I become exhausted by self-help's relentlessly upbeat tone. The only way is up. Things can only get better. I can't help but feel that what's being peddled is a flat-pack life lite, not the infinitely textured, often troubling and always fascinating thing that hits me day by day.

What is lacking is what might be called *wisdom*. I don't think this is something that can be derived in a lab. It comes from the careful, often exceptional, experience and reflection of those individuals who have been best at the art of living. It's like music, one of the subjects we'll consider here. Science and psychology can tell us a certain amount, and it can freshen up what has been learned before. However, Mozart and Moby can tell us a whole lot more besides.

In fact, Samuel Smiles might have made the same point. Many of his best ideas come from the ancient Greek philosophers, a source we'll draw much from too. They're often forgotten today, as we're so enamoured by the new. But what's new can also be a little green, a little untried and untested. My hope here is to reopen some of the oldest and deepest seams of insight, and to mine others that are newer but perhaps overlooked.

It turns out that there is more to life than success; that happiness, though desirable, is not enough. Those ideas are not big enough to inspire us to be all that we might be, to reach for our potential. They do not risk making weighty calls on our nature. They can't speak to the whole of our humanity, and thereby enlarge it.

If there's one theme that weaves its way through these 30 chapters (which, incidentally, can be read in succession or dipped in and out of), it's the approach known as virtue ethics. Virtues are those skills, habits and excellences that enable us to flourish, if we can nurture them. Virtue ethics does not seek definite answers, but rather a way of life, much like the musician who orientates their days around practice, learning and performance. It aims at those qualities that, got right, ensure you're heading more or less in the best direction – even though, for us humans, our exact destination is never entirely clear.

Simone Weil is one of the wise guides to the virtues that I've built into each chapter, and she put it roughly this way. We need both indicators of 'gravity' in life – the things that would drag us down – and indicators of 'grace' – the things that lift us up. Like Hercules, whom myth tells us came to a crossroads in life and had to make a choice, a sense of gravity and grace can help us decide what to commit to. In the following pages, I'm hoping to identify and suggest some of the indicators of grace to commit to, and of gravity to question.

I've tried to pick themes that are important, and are also perhaps unexpected, and in each case to find thoughts on them that are arresting, that might catch your imagination and encourage you to see things in a different light. The hope is that this then opens up a new step forward towards the good in life. Any of the end-of-chapter suggestions I've called 'steps' are not designed to change your life in an instant. Rather, they might yield an intimation of what is possible. It's such intimations that can take deep root. This principle of revelation by prompting a memory, reflection or insight is called 'love's knowledge', as expounded by Martha Nussbaum, another guide for us here. It's possible, that if a different dimension to life is awakened in you, or remembered, then life might take a slightly different course than it would otherwise have done.

I'd like to thank all those at Hodder who have worked on the book too, particularly Harry Scoble. There are some extraordinary individuals introduced in these pages, with some of the best ideas human beings have ever had about how to live well. I hope you find them as stimulating as I do.

Mark Vernon

1

Anger – the discomforting opportunity

ANGER *comes at the beginning of our exploration only because it begins with the letter 'a'. But that's also fortuitous because anger must be an integral, if arresting, part of any reflection on how to live well. Why? Well, we all feel it. We all have to contend with it.*

It can power an individual to great acts, breaking the hold of apathy and hopelessness. 'Anger in its time and place,' wrote the essayist and poet Charles Lamb, 'May assume a kind of grace.' But it can be the cause of your downfall too, in extremis being indistinguishable from the heat of madness. The art is to be capable of directing anger aright. And it is an art, for anger is always a complicated matter. Sure, righteous anger has much to do with justice; indignation with preserving your honour. But anger readily boils over into destructive rage.

Take Homer's most complex hero, Achilles. He is the Greeks most charismatic and passionate warrior, and yet he also performs repulsive acts born of blind fury. He avenges the death of his beloved, Patroclus, by vilely mutilating the body of Hector. Homer portrays this angry young man as at war with himself. When roused he can inspire an army. When self-pitying, he rages against fate. 'He will weep much, too late,' prophesies Nestor in the *Iliad*.

Ancient Greeks reflected on stories such as those of Achilles as a way of trying to train themselves. When anger took hold of them, the hope was that they might be guided by their cultivated, nobler instincts. Anger is a risky emotion. They knew that. But it is also a moral emotion with the capacity to redeem a life.

> *'The tygers of wrath are wiser than the horses of instruction.'*
> William Blake

Sigmund Freud (1856–1939)

Quick summary: The founder of psychoanalysis was a startling and arresting thinker in all sorts of areas. He can be thought of as reframing Socrates' question of how we should live by peering into the hidden aspects of ourselves, the dark forces that conspire to prevent us from living well.

Key text: His oeuvre is copious. *Civilization and Its Discontents* is a good place to start. I'd also recommend Jonathan Lear's philosophical introduction, *Freud* (2005).

Interesting fact: Once, when he tried to give up smoking, Freud confessed: 'It had served me well. . . as protection and weapon in the combat with life. So, I am better than before, but not happier.'

The protective emotion

One of Freud's insights illuminates why anger is so crucial an emotion to get right. Human beings routinely shift the blame for their difficulties, either from themselves to another, or from another to themselves. It's a deflecting strategy that protects them from feelings that are too much for them. A battered wife will rage against herself for the violence in her marriage, when the abusive husband is at fault: she prefers that to the greater fear that her marriage might fail. A politician will rage against the electorate when they lose an election, and so deny that, in truth, the electorate had sensed their personal flaws: that would be too much for them to cope with.

Misplaced anger means that the individual concerned never gets around to asking the right question. The wife doesn't ask, 'Should I leave?' but 'What's wrong with me?' The politician doesn't ask, 'What am I doing wrong?' but 'What's wrong with the voters?' But rage has to be redirected towards what Freud called the 'correct object' in order for the individual concerned to reach a better answer to the question, 'How should I live?'

An ugly emotion

Another problem is that anger is often regarded as an *ugly* emotion. Hence, Freud suspected, there is a great temptation to conceal your anger so you don't have to reveal yourself by its lights. He particularly noticed such a dynamic at work in the context of depression. (Sadness is more attractive than fury.) It's another way of thinking about how subtle an emotion anger can be.

An archetypal scenario concerns the relationship between a father and child. The child might feel anger at the father when they are told off, and simultaneously become guilty about those feelings, as a child also desires a father's love. So the anger is redirected, at themselves, an unconscious strategy that avoids the guilt, though with a damaging side-effect: the child develops

Figure 1 The couch as Freud arranged it when he saw his patients, at 20 Maresfield Gardens, Hampstead, London.

a habit of self-loathing: it's my fault. That precipitates a further convolution, as the angry self-criticism may well itself then be repressed, it too being unbearable. That, in turn, leaves the child with a pervasive, inchoate sense of unworthiness that can manifest itself as depression.

Blame and revenge

All sorts of complications can be added to this simplified story. (Freud was himself clear that the human psyche is never as simple as the psychoanalyst is tempted to imagine.) The anger can become closely associated with feelings such as blame and revenge. Conversely, it can lead to processes in which the individual identifies with the object of their fury: this might be what happens between a couple whose relationship consists of repeated cycles of fierce rows and equally passionate reconciliations. The two different emotions aren't actually opposite, but part of the same complex.

If that's how it can go wrong, how it can be put right might well come by understanding the sources of the original anger, though typically that is not a straightforward matter. If anger cloaks itself under many layers, they must be patiently removed, one at a time. Freud's technique for doing so was not to seek ready truths about the situation that purport to explain everything. That people often do offer such truths – it's my father's fault, it's my mother's – leads not to the richness of psychoanalysis but the shallowness of pop psychology. There is no quick closure, according to Freud. Instead, there are repeated attempts to find readings of what's going on, to propose possibilities that might hold some truth. Those possibilities are then tested against experience. If they make some sense, the analysis has removed a layer. If not, there's still more work to be done.

> 'Anger is never without an argument, but seldom with a good one.'
> Lord Halifax

The illuminating emotion

There is a fascinating story about anger, which Plato tells in his dialogue *The Republic*. It shows how anger is not necessarily an unwelcome part of life but can play a positive role too.

One day, a man called Leontius was walking back from the Athenian port, Piraeus, and he passed by some corpses, still fresh. They were lying at the executioner's feet. The sight revolted him, and he found himself caught up in an internal struggle. There was a part of him that wanted to look and stare. But another part was disgusted and thought he should turn away. He covers his face, Plato reports, and becomes angry at himself because he is not simply able to walk away from the grisly sight. He yearns to look. And eventually, his voyeuristic side wins out. He opens his eyes and steps towards the corpses.

But he is angry with himself for looking, and bitterly chastises his eyes: 'Look for yourselves, you evil wretches,' he mutters; 'take your fill of the beautiful sight.'

What does the story tell us? Although he fails to live up to his ideals, Leontius' moral sense is strong enough for him still to feel shame – shame expressed as anger. He is an individual who has done something distasteful. But, unlike the child who represses the guilt, he remains conscious of the nasty implications of his desire to stare. It's a side of his character that is ugly. He has done something revolting, and anger serves to remind him of that fact, which is advantageous. He has not acted well. But with anger's light, he has also not lost sight of the path to virtue.

Later in the day, back home, we can imagine him worrying about what happened, his anger again serving him well by not allowing the memory to fade. If he can cope with the discomfort, he might come to the conclusion that he had learned something about himself that day. He looked: he was drawn by the sight of mangled bodies. But he also remained indignant with himself while he stared. Like an individual who is in love and becomes jealous without cause, or a person at work who discovers that they have within them a nasty competitive streak, Leontius discovers a weakness in himself, but his awareness of that weakness is the first step towards tackling it. When he looks at himself, the sight is not pretty. And yet, he's discovered a truth about himself.

It takes anger to achieve that, because such self-reflection is painful and the ego has many strategies of defence, from justificatory self-righteousness to wilful self-ignorance. This kind of anger, which does not condemn the self but critiques it, provides the energy to challenge those defences.

Maybe another day, he passes by the same spot again, and does not look. Maybe another day again, further into the future, he passes by once more, and looks – only this time not out of a perverse pleasure but out of pity. He would have changed, and he might, then, thank the earlier anger. It had pained him. But without it, he would not have been aware that he could aspire to have a more admirable character.

He had to follow a fine line, for anger directed against oneself always risks becoming pathological. That is what worried Freud. It can ricochet off the defensive walls of the ego so that it becomes directed generally against the world. If Leontius had been too disgusted with himself, his anger might have been repressed, like the child's. He might have lashed out against others, as well as himself. That would have led to a tragic irony: the violence that revolted him caused him in turn to be violent. Anger can do that too. Similarly, a lover can be so horrified that their love for another provokes ugly feelings of unwarranted jealousy within them that, instead of battling the jealousy, they repress the feelings of love. They do not learn something about themselves but turn against their beloved.

'Love that is fed by jealousy dies hard,' Ovid wrote. But anger, though running the risk of backfiring, can lead to a better tomorrow when it is directed in the right way.

A moral emotion

What Freud and Plato alike imply is that anger is not simply a negative emotion, as is so readily assumed today. Some psychologists will tell you that it is bad for your health, raising your blood pressure and much worse, and that it should therefore be contained and dispersed, like an oil slick that would otherwise pollute the ocean. There have long been schools that have thought similarly about it. The ancient Greek Stoics argued that anger needs to be eliminated from any life that could be called wise. They were repelled by the angry individual's inflamed eyes, boiling blood and hissing breath. 'What can the mind be within if the image is so foul?' Seneca asked.

A certain kind of conversation with oneself is the key instrument for making a virtue out of this emotion. Freud called it *analysis*, the free expression of feelings and fears that the analyst interprets. It's a kind of reasoning, not in the sense of finding proof, but in the sense of understanding the causes. This kind of reason can illuminate the emotions and help us to discern what's best for us. It helps to ensure that the self-critique is constructive. It might be thought of as liberating anger, so that it becomes productive, as when anger fires the desire for justice. (It's worth remembering here that many sages are depicted as being angry, on occasion: Jesus in the Jerusalem temple when he overturned the tables of the money-changes; the Buddha, when one evening his monks did not respect their elders and betters.)

Plato has a helpful thought. He argued that the great task in life is to nurture the psyche so that it works harmoniously. One must educate one's anger, or 'make an ally of the lion', as he put it. A harmonious soul is one that will still feel anger, though it can use it, not be destroyed by it. A just individual will feel anger when they are forced to do something wrong, for example. This is anger as a moral emotion. Aristotle picked up on the theme too: 'It appears that anger does to some extent hear reason, but that it hears it wrongly,' he wrote. The challenge is to sharpen anger's hearing, so that the individual can detect the still small voice of virtue, even as the tumult of rage threatens.

There is a longstanding, and so presumably well-tested, tip for coping with anger. Mark Twain's version was: 'When angry, count four; when very angry, swear.' But as Freud realized, the real danger here is not anger per se, but the conflicts it causes and the individual's inability to cope with the associated feelings. An inner conflict troubled Leontius, though he found a way through it without lashing out. So in general, the way to avoid the destructiveness of anger is not to repress the feelings, or hold out in the hope they might be eliminated. That leads only to violence or depression. Rather, it is to learn to tolerate the discomfort and to regard anger as a source of revelation. As the chorus chants in one of Sophocles' plays, the gods punish the proud, but punishment brings wisdom.

So an angry experience is a discomforting opportunity. You might like to recall the last occasion on which you were angry – at your partner, in the car, at an injustice, with yourself. Time has elapsed since. You can now look at what happened more objectively. Be patient with yourself. Unpeel a layer. What injustices does the incident illuminate? What insights about yourself does it suggest?

Art – beyond consumption

ART is vital for human beings. Our ancestors, tens of thousands of years ago, developed a tendency to beautify things, simply for the aesthetic delight it gave. Even when objects had primarily practical purposes, they were extravagantly ornamented. A pestle was decorated with a feathery bird. An arrow head was far more elegantly shaped than the physics of flight and penetration alone required.

The extra effort cannot readily be explained by functionality, and yet it makes perfect sense if you see the human animal as a being who seeks to express itself – who seeks to connect with the world, to enter the flow of life, and thereby find a place in the world. We make objects beautiful to understand ourselves. Art, then, must be a part of any exploration of the good life.

> 'Life imitates Art far more than Art imitates Life.'
> Oscar Wilde

Art as expression

For the British philosopher R. G. Collingwood, the value of art in the good life is captured in one word: expression. However, he meant this in a particular way. Expressing yourself in art is not simply to give vent to your emotions or state of mind. A baby can do as much when it cries, though it would be ridiculous to call a mewling child artistic. Rather, expression proper is being able to give shape to and make sense of emotions and mental states. It is not just to cry, fear or laugh, but to *know what* it is to cry, fear and laugh. That insight is what the artist strives for, so as a form of self-knowledge, art is of enormous value for those seeking not just to live, but live well.

R. G. Collingwood (1889–1943)

Quick summary: Art, for Collingwood, is an object or event that gives expression to a thought or feeling, and which, by being shared, allows others to experience sympathetically that thought or feeling too.

Key text: *The Principles of Art* – and other writings, which are notable for combining artistic, intellectual and ethical insights.

Interesting fact: Collingwood was also a philosopher of history. He believed that imagination plays as key a part in the life of the historian as it does in the life of the artist, enabling him or her to explore the thoughts of other people.

Feeling fine

The artist is someone who pursues the question, What is it to feel? Artistic expression occurs when the artist devises a way of articulating an answer to that question, rendering what was inchoate clear. The artist embarks on a quest that leads to self-discovery. Why? Collingwood gives us the answer succinctly: 'Until a man has expressed his emotion, he does not yet know what emotion it is.' And he means expression in the sophisticated, not childish, sense.

That art is a process of discovery helps to explain why artists tend to use the same materials time and time again, and portray or represent the same subjects repeatedly. If Vincent van Gogh had painted sunflowers just once that would not be an *exploration* but a mere *representation*. So he paints them again, against turquoise, then royal blue, then blue-green and then yellow backgrounds. He paints them in full bloom and withering. In a letter to his brother, Theo, Vincent remarks, 'It is a kind of painting that rather changes in character, and takes on a richness the longer you look at it.' Life's richness richly expressed is what he sought.

Art and craft

A related theme that is important for Collingwood is the link between art and craft. He is sure that art requires craft, discipline, training and skill. To think otherwise is what he calls 'the sentimental notion that works of art can be produced by anyone, however little trouble he has taken to learn his job, provided his heart is in the right place'. In truth, it's only non-artists who would indulge such a notion, for every artist knows 'the vast amount of intelligent and purposeful labour, the painful and conscientious self-discipline, that has gone to the making of a man who can write a line as Pope writes it, or knock a single chip off a stone like Michelangelo'.

What Collingwood's pointing to here is *practical intelligence*, the kind of insight that arises only from wrestling with the stuff of art, its materials – paint, wood, paper, stone. For what it's worth, this relates to what I sense is wrong with much contemporary conceptual art. It's obvious characteristic is that conceptual artists themselves do not make anything. They produce ideas and then issue instructions to craftspeople or manufacturers who have the requisite skill to make the work. That says a lot, because, in truth, the best ideas can't be detached from the effort to realize them. This is practical intelligence, the kind of wisdom with materials that emerges from a long training of mind, body, character and engagement with a tradition. It's the part labour and discipline plays.

It might seem that this is a rather dispiriting view of art. After all, if art requires all that skill and effort – all that expressive sophistication – who beyond a rare few could claim to be an artist? It's undoubtedly true that great art is exceptional, born of exceptional individuals and cultural times. However, the emphasis on craft is also an invitation because it implies that artistic creativity can be *learned*. Few who learn the piano will be as good as Lang Lang. Few who take still-life classes will be able to draw like Leonardo. However, all who learn the piano will gain a greater appreciation of Lang Lang's brilliance, just as those who learn to draw will discover more about Leonardo. To do that much is to move away from being a mere consumer of art, and become someone who begins to understand it – from the inside. That is part of the value of art, as an expression of consciousness. It is an imaginative engagement with the world. That is what it means to be an artist.

> '*Art for art's sake, with no purpose, for any purpose perverts art.*'
> Benjamin Constant

A fuller consciousness

Collingwood connects his thoughts on art to an examination of what he calls 'the corruption of consciousness' that he diagnoses in the modern world. We can perhaps get a sense of what Collingwood means by considering a particular picture, *An Old Man and His Grandson*, by the Renaissance artist Domenico Ghirlandaio.

I'm indebted to Iain McGilchrist here, who in his book *The Master and His Emissary* explores how the workings of the brain link with artistic expression. McGilchrist's theme is what is known as laterality, the different functions of the left and right hemispheres. Laterality can be a metaphor that, though simplified, suggests something of what it is to have a full perception of the world, thereby achieving what Collingwood would call a truthful consciousness.

Here's the picture:

Figure 2 *An Old Man and His Grandson* (c.1490) by Domenico Ghirlandaio.

Let's look at three features of this painting:

1 **A synthesis of whole and specifics**
First, notice the sense of perspective through the window, not only in space, conveyed by the mountain, but also in time, conveyed by the winding road. This double sensibility is characteristic of the full flourishing of consciousness in the art of the Renaissance. McGilchrist describes a kind of movement, from right to left to right again. The right hemisphere first, as it were, picks up the whole of time and expansiveness of place the image shows; the left hemisphere then analyses the features of the image and then hands back those specifics to the right in order to produce the synthesis that the picture offers: the powerful sense of two real individuals standing in relation to the world and in 'lived time'.

Both hemispheres are required for this – the right's capacity to see the whole, the left's to discern the specifics. Bring the two aspects together, and the picture pulls at your imagination to see two human beings standing at a particular moment in relation to the broader context of their history. That's the genius of Renaissance art's expressiveness. It's a full

consciousness of what it is to be human; hence its
enduring appeal to us, centuries on.

2 **Togetherness and distance**
A second feature that also incorporates this dynamic
is the sense of empathy the picture produces, which
is one both of identification with the man and his
grandson, but also a sense of distance from them. We
view them knowing we're not them, but we view them
sympathetically. The distance between us and them
is appropriate to allow them to be themselves, and to
allow us to be with them too. Togetherness and distance.
A complete expression of consciousness.

The calm mood with which they meet is notable too.
It's not quite sadness. Rather it's the feeling that arises
from being wise about a situation. So the two seem
conscious of their mortality, the old man looking on
the young grandson, the young grandson wanting to be
with the old man through his life, implicitly knowing
he can't. The calmness arises from a conscious of the
mystery of beginnings and endings, of not being in
control of sources and causes. It's another manifestation
of finely explored expression.

3 **A living relationship**
A third feature is the way the picture conveys the
generations. These are not just two specimens from
one species, related by shared genes. Rather the picture
is of two distinct individuals whom we see in living
relationship, together forming a human whole – though
not losing their individuality in the process. It's another
balance.

Stepping back from the specifics of the picture, and
returning to Collingwood's insights: what Renaissance
art reminds us is that we live in an age that is losing
sight of these kind of balances, this fully expressive
capacity. Instead we tend to document our world not
live in it; we become confused about the self because

of an inability to achieve the right balance of closeness to and distance from others; and we prefer scientific generalizations rather than real human connections, provoking crises of meaning. If Collingwood is right, and as our appreciation of the works of the Renaissance like those by Ghirlandaio would seem to suggest, art can help us to rectify the corruption of consciousness.

A Step

The trick is to make the move from being a *consumer* of art to being, in some sense, a *maker* of art – which at a minimum is to appreciate the depth of expression in great works of art. Learning a new skill can be a way to do this – the skills that enable you to grapple with a novel, gaze at a painting, attend to some music. Write a sentence, play with paint, bash out some notes. That might lead you further to learning a craft. The aim is an appreciation of the articulacy, clarity and understanding conveyed in art, even if your own attempts are far from great. It's to be excited by the arts because they fire an excitement in you about what it is to be human. It is to feel part of that flow of life that reaches all the way back to our ancestors who made those first beautiful objects.

3

Beauty – as a guide in life

BEAUTY is not a fashionable subject. Toasters and lamps are beautifully designed. Dolphins and mountains are photographed in beautiful shades of blue. Celebrities and consumers alike spend a fortune on so-called beauty products. And yet, it's not hard to detect in our culture a deep suspicion of beauty.

We're inclined to suppose its artifice is only skin deep. The beautiful branding is a treacherous ploy. The beautiful smile deceives. Haunted by images of environmental degradation and the wasteful by-products of consumerism, we fear what beauty conceals, namely death and decay. The art world, too, which once specialized in creating beauty, now appears to have largely given up on it. It's as if that which is ugly, or at least ordinary, is more authentic and real. Beauty's power has become morally suspect too, because we know that even the worst human horrors – those of war – can be given a beautiful aura with the right lighting and cinematic tricks.

Beauty may very well imprison us as readily as it liberates us. But in discarding it utterly, we're at risk of losing an older notion – that beauty can speak to us of what is good.

> 'Beauty is all very well at first sight; but who ever looks at it when it has been in the house three days?'
>
> George Bernard Shaw

Iris Murdoch (1919–99)

Quick summary: Murdoch was interested in ethics because she believed that goodness is real and that we can seek it in life. It was, in fact, the way she believed we can now understand God.

Key text: *Metaphysics as a Guide to Morals* is a baggy text, with an intimidating title. *Existentialists and Mystics*, an anthology of her work, is a great place to start.

Interesting fact: She is better known for her novels, and for the brutality of her death from Alzheimer's.

. . . .

Iris Murdoch is our guide here. And for this reason: she knew that beauty must be connected to morality in order to be a constructive resource for the art of living. She didn't mean morality as in 'right and wrong', but rather morality as a kind of perception – seeing that which is true, and so desiring what is good more precisely. That's the link: beauty's appeal is that it draws us towards that which is beautiful, and that which is beautiful can be true, though we need to discern whether its allure is false, whether it's just skin deep, or rather enables us to live at depth. Beauty awakens the desire to do that, and our values must hone and shape what our desire awakens.

From this it follows that beauty speaks so powerfully to us because it promises something we desire, perhaps happiness or insight or fulfilment. This is why we love what is beautiful, and want to commit to it, often by possessing it – though we typically don't quite know what this might entail. You commit to your beautiful lover, though can't anticipate what 30 years together will bring. That lack of certainty about what beauty is promising, coupled to the way it speaks to our probably confused loves and longings, is why we will never conclusively agree about what is beautiful. Artists, designers, philosophers, lovers will continually debate it. That's the joy of the subject and its intractable nature.

Escape from Plato's Cave

Murdoch was a great interpreter of the philosopher Plato. It's from Plato she derives her ideas about how beauty, truth and goodness are linked. (They were also alike because Plato wrote great literature, just as Murdoch wrote great novels.)

Their common interest in beauty explains that too, because the truth of beauty, and the way it works, is arguably best explained by telling stories. They are imaginative exhibitions of the power of beauty. And there's one story that Plato told that is particularly powerful and still well known.

Figure 3 *Plato's Allegory of the Cave* (1604), engraving by Jan Saenredam, showing people being drawn by the beauty of the light.

The story appears in his dialogue *The Republic* and is called the 'Allegory of the Cave'. Plato describes how human beings who are unenlightened about the real nature of the world – who can't see its beauty – are like prisoners who are tied up in a darkened cave and are forced to stare at the back wall. On the wall they see shadows dancing against the grey confines of their enclosure. Most of these godforsaken souls take this world of shadows to be reality. However, some dare to catch a sideways glance, and what they see behind them is a surprise.

They see puppets and, behind the puppets, a fire. With that sight, they have a moment of realization: the back wall they had been staring at is not reality. Rather, what they are seeing are the shadows of the puppets, dancing against the grey confines of the cave. 'Behold!' Plato writes, 'Human beings living in an underground den. . . They see only their own shadows, or the shadows of one another, which are thrown on the opposite wall of the cave.'

To realize this is to take the first step towards a better understanding of the world: if you realize that what you often see is but shadows, then perhaps there is something more beautiful to seek and behold. The prisoner in the story becomes a pilgrim, and a second step is taken when, daring to progress a little more, they turn around again and edge towards the fire that is casting the shadows. This is compelling because light is beautiful, though frightening too, because it's fire. However, the promise of beauty brings courage, and so with nerves strengthened, the pilgrim shuffles around the fire and towards the mouth of the cave.

Something even more astonishing confronts them now: daylight. It too is beautiful and bewildering. Though, once accustomed to its spectacle, they move out of the dark, turn their heads heavenwards, and finally glimpse the source of all light: the sun. With that, the individual gains a proper perspective on the nature of things, if not a full understanding. It is one that could never have been intuited when they were staring at the wall at the back of the cave. Beauty has drawn them to it.

Kinds of beauty

Plato's allegory requires interpretation and it has been read in different ways. One interpretation might argue that the sun is like the truth that comes from scientific discovery. The insights are beautiful but abstract. They could never be grasped if all the individual relied on was the shadowy input of their senses; theories and testing, though, bring all things to light. So, under this interpretation, the path that Plato describes in the allegory of the cave is one that ascribes a very high value to science. 'Mathematics, rightly viewed, possesses not only truth, but supreme beauty – a beauty cold and austere, like that of sculpture', was Bertrand Russell's way of putting it.

However, Murdoch was quite clear that Plato himself meant more by his allegory. Mathematics is purifying; it awakens what Plato called an 'organ in the soul' that suggests a deeper way of seeing the truth. Mathematics and science clarify things because they discern patterns. But that's just the start of it. The shadowy life is one of grime and greys. The enlightened life is one of rich colour. It is the desire for beauty, of which the beauty of mathematics is a part, that enables the prisoner to overcome their fear, first of the shadows and then of the greater light that opens up before him. It's perhaps more like what Einstein said, when he reflected that 'behind all the discernible laws and connections, there remains something subtle, intangible and inexplicable. Veneration for this force beyond anything that we can comprehend is my religion.'

There is a mystical element that opens up with this aesthetic experience too. As the pilgrim leaves the confines of the cave, they come to experience the world as much bigger than themselves. Reality comes to be recognized as conceptually wider than can be grasped with reason alone: perceiving truth is an exercise of the imagination as well as of science. It requires metaphor and allusion, as well as logic. The quest for beauty naturally reaches out for these things. It's why stories are so important.

It also suggests that truth has a transcendent and metaphysical quality. This is why Murdoch thought that a useful way of talking about the divine in the modern world, and of addressing the religious impulse, is to talk about the Good, rather than God. What Plato's allegory leaves us with is a sense of the tremendousness of being able to appreciate such a thing as truth at all, if only obliquely. And we appreciate it because it is both beautiful and good. It's a compelling story. It appeals to an intuition that seems right, namely that to understand what is true is to see more clearly, to have cultivated a penetrating mind, a deeper experience of things that was awakened by beauty.

> '*The awful thing is that beauty is mysterious as well as terrible. God and devil are fighting there, and the battlefield is the heart of man.*'
> Fyodor Dostoevsky

Beauty in practice

We can think about how beauty works in practice by looking at an experience everyone has had: falling in love. We spot someone across a room and are instantaneously attracted to them. It may be their physical presence, or it may be something more mysterious that they radiate and that draws us – their soul. But suddenly we see them. The rest of the room disappears into the background. And we want that beauty, to make it our own, so that our lives can gain from it, can become part of it.

It's an unsettling experience because it also implies that your life as it currently exists may not be as full, as true, as it could be. Like Plato's pilgrim emerging from the cave, there's more than you realized. The French novelist Stendhal put it another way, when he noted that beauty is the *promise* of happiness – the promise of a different future. If beauty unleashes our desire, it does so without us quite knowing what it will lead to, what it will disclose, what it will transform.

Beautiful stories

'A deep motive for making literature or art of any sort', Murdoch said, 'is the desire to defeat the formlessness of the world and cheer oneself up by constructing forms out of what might otherwise seem a mass of senseless rubble.'

So here's the link between beauty and pattern: it's found in the way we tell of our lives. If beauty is a prompt to seek the truth – because it draws us to the truth – then the accounts we have about ourselves and the world are truth-seeking and truth-revealing exercises. When they are committed to the page, and judged in some way for their aesthetic value too, those accounts become literature. It's what Shakespeare did in his plays, Montaigne in his essays, Plato in his philosophy, Murdoch in her novels.

There is no one type of literature, of course. Murdoch pointed out that literature uses all sorts of devices to reflect on life – fiction, masks, play, pretence, imagination, story, reason, logic. But there is a sense in which great literature is always beautiful. That's what makes it great.

Great literature is also rare, but the act of giving an account of life is something we all engage in, as we are all the tellers of our lives: 'We are constantly employing language to make interesting forms out of experience which perhaps originally seemed dull or incoherent,' Murdoch says. We do it every time our partner asks us how our day was, and we respond with enthusiasm; we do it every time a friend enquires how we are, and we feel that our lives contain some beauty worth relating.

So this is something to do more consciously. When next asked, make something of your day. Seek out its moments of beauty and try to speak of them. Avoid sentimentality and fantasy. Think about the patterns. With that effort, beauty could be drawing you towards something that is true.

4

Community – or the ties that free us

THE word 'infant' conceals a profound truth about what it is to be human. Infant does not mean 'young' or 'adorable', 'screaming thing' or 'puking thing'. It means 'one who cannot speak'. The great task of a parent, then, is to give their child a language – and that does not just mean the words to demand more orange juice, or others to convey thanks. It means an entire framework of meaning, one carried in a language. With it, we've a chance of making the world feel like home.

To speak is to belong with others who speak the same language. It is to be understood, to be heard, to be chastened, to be loved. As the deaf mute, Helen Keller, recalled when, as a child, she learned the word *water*: 'That living word awakened my soul, give it light, joy, set it free!' She was no longer alone. She knew herself as part of a community. Community is integral to the good life; learning how to live in communities, part of the art. Being able to speak, to cease being an infant, is the first step most of us take in the process, though only the first.

Saint Benedict (480–550)

Quick summary: Benedict was probably a Roman nobleman. He first became a hermit and was then moved to set up a community of monks on the mountaintop of Monte Cassino in southern Italy.

Key text: The Rule of Saint Benedict, a lucid document that does not only describe how a community might be run, but also contains insights into how human community works.

Interesting fact: Benedict is a shadowy historical figure, known more through legend than fact. The name itself means 'blessed one', and it's possible the Rule is a bundle of ideas, gathered together from disparate sources.

> *'Those only are happy (I thought) who have their minds fixed on some object other than their own happiness; on the happiness of others, on the improvement of mankind.'*
>
> John Stuart Mill

Benedict's Academy

The story of the establishment of Benedict's community carries an illuminating coincidence of history. Benedict moved to Monte Cassino around the year 529, occupying an old temple dedicated to Apollo and turning it into a monastery dedicated to Christ.

Figure 4 Saint Benedict's community house today, on Monte Cassino.

It so happens that, in the same year, Plato's Academy was finally closed in Athens. For 900 years, it had been not just a powerhouse of philosophy and ideas, but also a community too. The old philosophers committed themselves to a way of life, alongside the rigours of thought. They aimed together to transform themselves, realizing that, like infants, it is only possible to become all they might be as humans by learning in a community.

Benedict's new community of monks was a remaking of that tradition. Like the old philosophers, these new seekers after wisdom wore cloaks and carried staffs. They balanced their daily life by mixing up study, work, prayer and recreation in equal measures. Plato had once commented that the task he and his brethren were engaged in was no ordinary matter, but was concerned with the right way to live. Benedict, too, was concerned with how his monks could live in a virtuous way that would provide an example to the wider Christian society.

But what does the Rule say about community?

Obedience and rules

One thing that immediately strikes you about the Rule is its practicality. It is not just written in a simple way, but is concerned with the basic things of a common life. There is a marked stress on obedience, for example, backed up by physical punishment. To be frank, that element is harder to stomach today. But there was a practical aim here: to balance the interests of the individual with the well-being of the community. Roman society was collapsing; the barbarians were waiting at the frontiers. The discipline of Benedict's communities was one reason they attracted a following. The emphasis on punishment must be set against the lawlessness of the times.

We can learn something from the stress on obedience, however. Think of it this way. Communities embody customs and traditions, standards and rules. These give them character, certainly, but more they become the means by which individuals within them can learn skills and virtues for life. The Scottish philosopher Alasdair MacIntyre has called them 'practices'. Communities, according to his understanding, should be conceived of broadly: the members needn't all live in one place. Violinists, chess masters and football players belong to *extended* communities of violinists, chess masters and football players, and it is only by belonging to those communities that they become excellent in those activities. It is by having a shared purpose that these practices take on their meaning for us, and deliver their delights.

This requires obedience – to the rules of football, say, or the critique of other violinists. To learn what move works best at a certain moment in a game of chess requires a kind of submission. Or as MacIntyre has it, in relation to baseball: 'If, on starting to play baseball, I do not accept that others know better than I when to throw a fast ball and when not, I will never learn to appreciate good pitching let alone to pitch.' Obedience can, in fact, be liberating, enabling you to do something you'd never have achieved without it.

Beer and gossip

Another feature of Benedict's Rule is the small details he provides on how monks should relate to one another. There is a discussion, for instance, about how much wine monks should drink. Not none, 'because monks in our times cannot be persuaded of this'; but not too much either, because 'wine maketh even wise men fall off'. There's also a wise set of instructions about 'restraint of speech': gossip and grumbling are expressly frowned on, for as the book of Proverbs wryly has it, 'In a flood of words you will not avoid sin.'

What Benedict is on to here are the virtues that can only be learned together. They have been called 'civic virtues'. For example, how much should you drink on a Friday night when out on the town so that you can enjoy yourself but do not destroy the pleasure of others? There is no fixed amount; it's an art not a science, a virtue that French communities seem to teach quite naturally, and British ones do not. Similarly, with gossip. Gossip can, in fact, be a great way to bring people together, by sharing a common complaint. But gossip is also a destroyer of community. It's a question of balance – about which Benedict clearly veered on the side of caution.

Civic virtues are only learned in community – by sitting alongside a stranger on the bus, sharing a public park, going to community schools, using fitness clubs with others. As the US political philosopher Michael Sandel has pointed out, it is for this reason that today's divided society is such a worrying phenomenon. People live in gated housing developments. Ensconced behind their fences, and guarded by CCTV cameras, they stymie their chance to learn civic virtues because they don't rub up against fellow citizens. The result is that fear tends to win out over trust; rudeness over politeness.

To live in a community, Sandel continues, is to change 'habits of the heart'. That's the level at which good citizenship takes place, at which the common good is explored. For example, universal health care comes about when citizens realize that they have a duty of care to one another; mitigating climate change comes about when citizens' attitudes towards the planet change, as they now know the planet belongs to others too.

More broadly, a politics of the common good would work to rebuild the infrastructure of public life: municipal not membership health clubs, better public transport not more private cars, state not private schools, and so on. Such a shift can't happen overnight, but it starts when we learn to exercise our civic virtues once again. It's a notion of common life that is very much in the spirit of Benedict.

> 'We started off trying to set up a small anarchist community, but people wouldn't obey the rules.'
> Alan Bennett

Stability

My own experience of living in one particular community
highlights another element that Benedict knew to be important.
It was a kind of commune, seven people living together in a
house in north London. There was nothing very frugal about it:
the house itself was rather handsome and had a large garden.
And our commitment together was not onerous. It involved
cooking, cleaning and caring for each other: the ethos was as
much practical as idealistic. We had separate working lives
and looked after each other perhaps as relatively independent
sisters and brothers. But there was one quality the house had
that I think was key: stability.

It was provided by four members of the community who
had lived in the house for a long time: I lived there for about
five years; they'd been there for thirty. Their commitment to
the place, the routines and habits they'd built up, provided
the stability. They were small things, such as the little rituals
about how to do the washing up – glasses first, pans last. When
guests came there was a rule that, if the subject of conversation
veered towards something a guest might find uncomfortable,
someone would say: 'Did you see the post box was closed up
again today.' They were the kind of customs any family will have
too. 'No computer games at the table.' 'Drinks are served in the
Green Room at seven.' We noticed them only because we were
consciously trying to live together in a community.

Saint Benedict knew that stability was crucial for his
monks. It takes time to learn to live in community, time in
which you must stay put. The existence of the Rule was
much to do with stability too, to provide the patterns of life
into which everyone can fall. Rules needn't be terribly complex.
They are mostly about practical things, like eating together.
I realized that it was the very practical ways of nurturing
stability that the others who lived in the commune implicitly
understood.

Friendship and goodwill

What community helps you to realize is that life is a collective not individualistic project. It's a kind of friendship. Friendship tells us that we are not billiard balls that collide and rebound. Neither are we like drops in the ocean, which lose their identity as they dissolve in the larger mass of water. Rather, we are a fine suspension *of* one another, *in* each other. We are dependent and independent. The good life, witnessed to by community, arises from both principles.

When we don't have a sense of community, we live with each other as if we were foreigners; we don't live in communities but in companies of strangers. It's a view of life that struggles to believe in social justice, say, because that involves recognizing that my own good is implicitly caught up with the lives of others.

When thinking about extended communities, this kind of friendship is manifest as a reciprocal goodwill shared by those who know they belong to one another. Goodwill is what makes community possible, and the community shows and nurtures a corporate sympathy. Individuals are bound together not primarily by rules, though they may well feel an obligation to one another and rules can be a guide, but fundamentally by bonds of concern.

We all live in a number of communities, some located in particular places – families, schools, towns; others in virtual spaces, held together by shared pursuits, be it work, hobbies or citizenship. It's worth spending a few minutes doing a 'community audit', to gain a sense of what your personal communities give you, and what you give them. They can be represented by circles, drawn like a Venn diagram. Some will be large, others small. A few will overlap or be separate. One or two might envelop the whole of your life.

It is striking how many communities we still belong to, even in an age that otherwise thinks of itself as individualistic. And as you look, assess yours by Benedict's standards. What role does obedience, gossip, virtue and stability play in them?

5

Earth – our island home

THE *environment has become a substantial problem in ethics. But not in the way most people think. The question is not whether global warming is manmade and occurring. It is. Neither is it whether humankind should be doing more to care for this island home. We should. Rather, the problem is that we simply don't have the ethical language – or better, the moral imagination – that is strong enough to make a difference.*

This was demonstrated by the failure of Copenhagen, the conference in 2009 that was supposed to outline a global fix. As Mary Midgley, our philosopher-guide here, explains: the ethical framework we deploy for thinking about the environment 'leads either to denial, and the difficulty of accepting the facts about climate change, or to a desire to postpone the implications, "Lord, make me green but not yet."' So what's gone wrong, and can it be put right?

'The world is a living thing that contains within itself all the living things.'
Plato

Mary Midgley (b. 1919)

Quick summary: Over a long career, Midgley has argued that
modern moral philosophy goes disastrously wrong when it
conceives of human beings as rational minds in machine bodies,
instead of as a particular kind of social animal that is integral in
nature.

Key text: *Beast and Man* is the book in which she aims to bring
human nature back to the centre.

Interesting fact: She is a careful reader of Charles Darwin,
arguing that the selfish gene version of evolution is one that
would have appalled him. He too believed human beings to be
fundamentally social animals.

Gaia nature

Midgley's environmental philosophy is based on the
concept of Gaia. It's an holistic approach to thinking about
the Earth as a self-sustaining natural system. Every facet of
the planet – from the continental drift of plate tectonics, to
the carbon cycle at the heart of life, to the consciousness that
intuits the intrinsic grandeur of nature – can be viewed as the
workings of a single organism.

It contrasts dramatically with the view of ourselves as, as
Midgley phrases it, 'detached, spiritual beings, securely based
outside an inert, passive material world, owning it and free
to shape it for our own purposes'. This individualistic ethic
was born in the seventeenth century, when the first scientists
imagined the world as a gigantic mechanism through which
human minds floated. The world as machine was a fantastically
successful metaphor. With it flowed everything from Newton to
DNA.

However, the evolutionary story of our emergence paints a
very different picture, as does the notion of Gaia. Hence, today,
Midgley explains:

'We live in a different world – a world no longer made out
of solid little billiard-balls but (apparently) more or less out of

energy – forces and fields. Most of us, too, now see humankind itself as something naturally evolved, not as a distinct spiritual tribe colonizing alien matter.'

The scientific stance

The trouble is that, although the science has changed, the imagination of scientists – and by extension, ourselves – hasn't yet changed too. Science still proceeds by encouraging scientists to distance themselves from the world. Being objective is regarded as the quintessentially scientific stance. The knowledge we value the most, which we refer to as 'scientific', commands our respect for the very reason that it treats the natural world as a series of alien objects.

That might not seem surprising when it comes to studying volcanic ash in the atmosphere, or sulphur-eating life forms on the bed of the ocean, though Gaia asks us to contemplate our connection to these phenomena too. But we might get a sense that something is wrong when, say, that rich flow of coloured experience we call consciousness is studied as if it were the by-product of electrical activity in a piece of meat labelled the brain. Such reductionism clearly has got something fundamentally wrong.

It's called *materialism*, the view that at base the world is made of physical, inanimate, intrinsically worthless stuff. And, as has been observed, the trouble with materialism is not that it *over*values the material but that it *under*values the material. Hence, the throw-away nature of consumer culture. There are more positive signs, however. No longer do physicists conceive of the world as made out of particles in constant motion, but as a great web of energy, connections and possibility. Werner Heisenberg, one of the fathers of quantum physics, put it like this: 'The modern interpretation of events has very little resemblance to genuine materialistic philosophy: in fact, one may say that atomic physics has turned science away from the materialistic trend it had during the nineteenth century.'

The living world

This new science recalls the older imagination that envisaged the Earth as living. It's a way of looking at the planet that resonates not only with changes in physics but with the extraordinary pictures of the Earth sent back from space missions. Recall the iconic images of Earthrise from the moon. The blasted rock and dust of the Moon's surface is in the foreground – grey, dead and inert. Then, over the horizon, like an opening flower, emerges the Earth. Gaia it is not just gleaming and vividly coloured. It looks alive, even cheerful.

This is not a planet from which to feel alienated, as the materialist world view requires. For all its explanatory success, such a philosophy cannot accommodate the most basic sense we have about reality. But with Gaia, Midgley argues – a living Earth, acting to preserve itself – we find 'a long-needed context, a background that explain[s] human activity as part of a larger whole'. There is, however, resistance to the new imagery. The notion of Gaia itself, with its overtones of the mother-goddess, is shocking. But should it be? It is entirely appropriate, Midgley believes:

'That sense of wonder and gratitude is clearly what the Greeks had in mind when they named the Earth Gaia, the divine mother of gods and men. They never developed that naming into full humanization. They never brought Gaia into the scandalous human stories that they told about other gods – stories which, in the end, made it impossible to take those gods seriously at all. But the name still expresses their awe and gratitude at being part of that great whole.'

If that feels like too much to stomach, it could well be because the shift from the materialistic world view is a substantial leap too.

'Nature proceeds little by little from things lifeless to animal life in such a way that it is impossible to determine the exact line of demarcation.'

Aristotle

Gaia's revenge

Gaia theory is predominantly the work of the UK scientist James Lovelock. Since he developed the notion that the Earth is comprised of overlapping, reflexive systems, he's become closely associated with environmental concerns. But while the science leads Midgley to imagine human beings as at home in the world, Lovelock's imaginary is more troubling. Human beings are bit players on the planet, he says, and we've become an irritant. Global warming, he continues, is Gaia's way of scratching that itch, like a parasite that overstays its welcome, and her purging of the human tickle will not turn out well for us.

Lovelock envisages that, by the end of the twenty-first century, the world population of roughly 7 billion will be reduced to 1 billion. He's convinced that climate change will suddenly tip into 4 degrees plus of warming – history, he points out, shows the planet's climate systems don't rise and fall smoothly. Moreover, he says, there's no saving the planet: the very idea witnesses to human hubris. We can only mitigate the effects of the coming fiery furnace. Like Zeus, Gaia will act with an unremitting necessity that mocks human suffering.

Lovelock explains: 'Our ignorance of the Earth system is great; we know little more than an early 19th-century physician knew about the body.' And it leads him to conclude that, like the wiser physicians of the early 19th century who allowed nature to take its course, so too we might be better leaving Gaia alone and allowing her to adapt and recover. She has survived equally challenging eventualities in her three billion years of history.

Radical politics

At this point, it's necessary to offer a warning. For Lovelock's bleak view of the imminent future can excuse a truly horrific politics. I've heard it articulated in radical green groups. The logic, more or less consciously articulated, is that if calamity is just around the corner, then that justifies a suspension of ethics as usual. If you believe millions are going to die as a result of disruptive calamity, and probably billions need to die because of population overload, then the leap to positively desiring a holocaust becomes quite small. There are folk who feel we may as well 'bring it on', or at least offer little resistance to the carbon car crash of humanity. Terror is inevitable anyway.

What's doubly striking is that the individuals welcoming the end times are major beneficiaries of the energy-intensive way of life that has brought us to this moment. Without it, they would never have heard of Lovelock, or be able to share their dark fantasies with kindred spirits on the internet.

My reading of this eco-extremism is that there's a kind of displaced guilt going on. Those who must die, those whose freedom can be sacrificed, are a kind of scapegoat for our ecological sins. There's also the religious logic of apocalypticism at play. This is the myth of redemptive violence, the idea that at various points in history things get so bad that only the havoc wreaked by the Four Horseman will suffice to put it right.

And a third element I sense is the consolation to be found in holding something as certain, in this case the science that apparently predicts collapse in our lifetimes, possibly within a decade. The inherent uncertainty of the science of the future, for which the slightest changes in the initial conditions provoke massively different outcomes, has passed by these followers of disaster-science, as has Lovelock's observation that our knowledge of planet Earth and her systems is characterized mostly by ignorance.

A Step

A less misanthropic way forward, however, is possible. There are, of course, lots of practical matters to consider – from lagging homes to greener energy. However, there is another element, a more imaginative exercise.

It is to nurture the Gaia view of the world, to see ourselves not as independent but dependent; not as matter-machines but as living entities; not as means and ends but parts and wholes. Midgley sums it up in this way: 'We need the vast world, and it must be a world that does not need us; a world constantly capable of surprising us, a world we did not program, since only such a world is the proper object of wonder.'

The hope then is this. Our view of ourselves and our planet can change. Caring for the environment can come as naturally as caring for our children because we naturally feel part of them. The materialistic philosophy of our times can loosen its grip on us, with the result that the world will be an entirely different place. 'Big, dramatic changes in the world tend to seem quite natural after they have happened, yet look impossible in advance,' Midgley concludes. 'This is surely because the imagery of our own times grips us so powerfully.' It is this imagery that she asks us to critique and then move beyond.

6

Forgiveness – and having a future

IF you're capable of forgiveness, you have a future. If you're intent on revenge, you're tied to reliving the grievances of the past. If you can't absolve those who have wronged you, you're caught in cycles of blame. The unforgiving way of life can't look forward because it can only look back. The individual who can't forgive is an individual whose eyes have been removed from the front of their head and transplanted into the back of their skull.

So forgiveness seems desirable, and good practice for life. But it is not easy. In fact, those things that are easy to forgive barely need forgiving – a few minutes' lateness for dinner; the email languishing unanswered in your inbox. They are those transgressions that are, in truth, 'not a problem'; when wronged in these ways we forget them as much as forgive them. So it's the hard cases that are the important ones – the wounding incidents and raw memories that debilitate our ability to live well. Has philosophy much to say about that?

> 'Everyone says forgiveness is a lovely idea, until they have something to forgive.'
> C.S. Lewis

Jacques Derrida (1930–2004)

Quick summary: The French philosopher is known for deconstruction, the approach to ideas that tries to unpick their tightest knots. Take hospitality. We say to our guests, 'Make yourself at home.' And yet, if they literally did that – if they moved the furniture around and took down the pictures – we'd want to be rid of them. So what is hospitability? Derrida asks.

Key text: He discusses forgiveness in *On Cosmopolitanism and Forgiveness*, noting that forgiveness is a political issue in a plural world: world leaders now ask forgiveness of minorities or the vanquished with striking regularity.

Interesting fact: When Cambridge University awarded Derrida an honorary degree, it led to such protests that the award was delayed, though eventually granted.

Forgiving the impossible

What Derrida noticed about forgiveness was precisely what C. S. Lewis noticed too: things that are easy to forgive barely need forgiving, whereas the things that we most need to forgive seem impossible to absolve. Consider the way a parent forgives their child hour by hour, day by day. The kid knocks hot tea on to the carpet; it weeps inconsolably through the night; it elbows Mum in the eye so that she weeps. And Mum doesn't really feel she has anything to forgive at all; and Dad doesn't really blame the child to start with. Parents absorb the disruptions that offspring bring to their lives, they accept them as intrinsic to being a parent. There's really no forgiving to be done.

But now consider how the parent would respond should something happen to their child. If a child is abused or injured by another adult, we're moving into the difficult territory of the *unforgivable*. If a youngster is killed, we'd think it truly remarkable were a parent to forgive the perpetrator, and perhaps unbelievable.

Lesser sins are quite enough to make forgiveness impossible too. Who would risk criticizing the parenting skills of even their best friend? We rightly hesitate to do so, recognizing that our critique, though gentle, might be unpardonable. It'd be too easy to venture something that once uttered would become unforgettable, un-withdrawable, and so very hard to forgive.

So Derrida has a good point. True forgiveness looks like it might be an impossible task because what we do forgive is readily forgivable – or perhaps, in truth, when we think we've forgiven, we've really just forgotten how the injury first felt.

The lightness of forgiveness

It seems a bleak conclusion to reach as, today, we're quite routinely told that forgiveness is vital to a happy life. This is the therapeutic notion of forgiveness. Individuals who have been caught up in the horrors of war are advised that they will achieve closure only if they can forgive their captors or rapists and the killers of their comrades.

There is a truth in this advice. It can be cathartic to acquit an enemy and let bygones be bygones. The promise is a new future. It's not for nothing that resentment is often described as a weight, and when you can put that weight down, or let it fall from your shoulders, the reward is an experience of lightness and liberation.

As for the little forgivenesses of daily life – the minor offences, the modest hurts – a therapist may well have techniques that help you let go too. They may encourage you not to over-dramatize what's happened, but to see it objectively, as part of a bigger picture. They will ask you to see things from the perpetrator's point of view. They may remind you of times you've yourself been forgiven, and ask whether you cannot offer the same. They may suggest enacting the forgiveness you seek to give, thereby actualizing it in reality.

But are these strategies not so much for forgiving, as forgoing the desire for revenge, lessening retributive feeling in order to make way for leniency? If you can see it from the perpetrator's point of view, then maybe there was not so much to forgive anyway.

And perhaps part of the reason why true forgiveness might be impossible is that something else is demanded to right wrongs – not forgiveness or forgetting, but justice. If someone has killed or maimed, then are we not right to seek their punishment? Seen in this light, simply to forgive looks like a moral failure. How can we honour those who have died at another's hand if no one pays the price? Even in less serious cases, such as forgiving accusations made by a friend about your parenting, there is an important sense in which what is said is said: presumably it came from a genuine thought or impulse and so can't be undone. If I blurted out that your children's behaviour is appalling, I've spoken the truth as I see it, and confessed I think you are a poor parent too. It's only right that you should seek a fairer assessment of your parenting skills, and never again from me.

The world before forgiveness

It's perhaps for reasons like these that the ancient philosophers did not actually pay much attention to forgiveness: it's not included in any list of virtues and wasn't an ethical concern. They sensed that *justice* was the real issue.

When they did raise issues that seem close to forgiveness, they worked with a different concept from ours. Today we'd define forgiveness as pardoning someone despite the fact that they are responsible for what they've done wrong. Aristotle, for one, discussed forgiveness in relation to pardoning someone when they are *not* responsible for their wrong action. Hence, he writes: 'There is pardon, whenever someone does a wrong action because of conditions of a sort that overstrain human nature, and that no one would endure.' But if that person cannot be blamed, because their nature has been 'overstrained', or because the conditions they faced were not endurable, then it's not forgiveness they need but understanding. We'd look for the causes of their wrongdoing. Perhaps it was their upbringing, their socio-economic disadvantage, the wiring in their brain.

Co-operative pressure

It's striking that the science of evolution tells a dramatically different story again. The latest idea is that forgiveness is actually a natural thing for human beings to do. For if we could not forgive the wrongs others do us, then we would soon stop co-operating with them. Forgiveness, here, is defined as not retaliating when an opponent makes a selfish move against you. But because it's easy to imagine situations in which it would be sensible to forgive them their selfishness, particularly if at some future point we are likely to gain from them – the parent 'forgives' the child because the child carries their genes – then forgiveness is precisely what the human animal has learned. It's really in our own interests.

Hence, we tend not to seek redress for the ills that befall us, and so are able to co-operate in ways that are quite extraordinary compared with other creatures in the natural world. Revenge killings among *Homo sapiens* are rare compared with other intelligent species. Forgiveness could, in fact, be the key to our evolutionary success. Without it, there'd be no cities, no economy, no traditions because there'd be no extensive co-operation. Further, it could be said that forgiveness is morally good: it's written into our genes and brings about positive outcomes, namely reconciliation.

But I suspect that this is where the evolutionary ideas go wrong. If Derrida's right, the science is focusing only on those things that are easy to forgive, and so don't really require forgiveness at all. If I can see it's in my own interests to forgive someone, then am I really forgiving them at all, and not rather exempting them? It's like the incidents a parent excuses in their child. The tricky cases are the ones that really require forgiveness because, as they fester, they ruin our lives and deny us a future. It's those that are so hard. Also, while the human animal may be extraordinarily co-operative, we are also extraordinarily violent – the only animal to threaten its fellows with mutually assured nuclear destruction, we shouldn't forget. That's how impossible true forgiveness is.

> *'True reconciliation does not consist in merely forgetting the past.'*
> Nelson Mandela

Prodigal returns

We can take the issue deeper by turning to another source of ideas about forgiveness in Western culture: Christianity. In fact, Christianity could be said to be the movement that introduces the notion of forgiveness into our civilization. The Greeks and Romans didn't much go in for it. But after Christianity, forgiveness became a state of being that everyone should seek, because everyone falls short at some point or another. Worse still, in the Christian analysis, the whole of humanity is infected with what came to be called 'original sin', the apparently intractable tendency to cause unforgivable injury to others.

One of the striking stories that Christians remember is the parable told by Jesus of the prodigal son. It tells of a man who had two male offspring. One day, the younger son asked his father for his share of the family inheritance. The father was remarkably obliging: there and then,

Figure 6 Rembrandt van Rijn, *The Return of the Prodigal Son* (1662). Rembrandt depicts the 'forgiveness' offered the prodigal son by his father.

he divided his property and handed half over to the impetuous youth. The young man promptly packed up his possessions and left for a foreign country where he 'wasted all his money in wild living'. A bad famine spread across the land and the impecunious son was left with nothing to eat. He ends up in a pig pen, eating the husks of the unclean animals. And then he comes to his senses. Even his father's workers eat better than he does, he reflects. He decides to return home and ask his father to be treated not as a son but as one of the slaves.

As the story details, the father sees his son returning from afar. And he runs out to greet him, with profound and moving affection. Moreover, the father doesn't even hear the son's request to be taken on as a slave. Instead, he throws a party. The fattened calf is slain, and they celebrate.

The twist in the tale comes when the older son protests. He's never been given a goat to share with his friends! So how come his brother, the spendthrift, is treated thus. The brother is so angry that he cannot enter the house. Who can blame him? But the father comes out again, and tells the elder boy that they share everything. So he too should celebrate. 'Your brother was dead, but he is now alive. He was lost and has now been found.'

Love and forgiveness

It's easy to read the story as one of forgiveness, and dramatic forgiveness at that. By spending his inheritance, the younger son has forfeited his future. He no longer deserves to be called a son. Does not his father forgive him? Is not the brother encouraged to do the same? Is this not a case of difficult forgiveness achieved, the almost impossible kind – which is why the elder brother finds his father's party-throwing so outrageous?

But what's arresting about the story is that forgiveness is not discussed at all. The parable does not have the father forgive the son, nor forget his misdemeanours. In fact, the son does not even ask for forgiveness, but rather makes a request to be taken on as a slave, a request the father simply ignores.

It's as if the biblical account foresaw Derrida's analysis. True forgiveness is impossible. That's what the son realizes. But what that makes way for is something else entirely, a completely new dimension. It's called love. This is the dynamic that was never lost in the father's regard for his son. It allows forgiveness to simply be sidestepped. Hence, the sheer extravagance of the story. It feels like a moral affront, because according to the logic of forgiveness it is. 'Hurry and bring the best clothes and put them on him,' calls the father. 'Give him a ring for his finger and sandals for his feet.' That's what the elder son can't comprehend. Trapped in the past, and unable to forget, he is driven crazy.

What's being suggested is that when we think we've seen truly impossible forgiveness, we've actually seen something else at work. A mother 'forgives' the terrorist murderer of her son. A prisoner of war 'forgives' his torturer. It's not so much that they forgive what is unforgivable, let alone that they seek justice or revenge – or can forget. Rather, they are still able to love, and hence to live with what has happened in a way that allows them to look forward. It's an astonishing feat. It demands courage, effort and vision. It changes lives. Hence Christians refer to love as the highest virtue.

At the risk of sounding like a preacher, you might like to read the parable of the prodigal son again yourself: Luke 15: 11–24. (It's such an important story that it can't be left to the preachers.) What's really going on there? Not, I'd say, forgiveness.

7

Freedom – by giving stuff up

WHAT *does freedom mean to you? More choice? More time? More opportunities? Freedom has become a quality that defines why we believe it's good to live today. Do we not enjoy more freedoms now than perhaps at any other time in history? Is not now the best time to be alive?*

So why is it so easy for these choices, time and opportunities to feel like a burden. I remember once sitting down in a diner, and asking for some eggs and toast. The sun glinted off the plastic table surface as the waitress smiled and enquired whether I wanted my eggs easy-over, sunny-side up, scrambled, poached, boiled, as a white or yellow omelette. . . Then there was the choice of bread, white, brown, rye, malted, plain, toasted, fried. . . The choices alone were so replete that I quite lost my appetite. The diner didn't offer me culinary freedom but a tyranny of choice.

Ivan Illich (1926–2002)

Quick summary: Illich was a kind of freelance philosopher, who worked both in Europe and the Americas. A great inverter of ideas, he believed that serious study was done around the dining table with friends as much as in the library with books.

Key text: In *Deschooling Society* (1971), he argued that education was becoming an industrial process, with schools and universities resembling factories – producing persons, if not parts, for the economic machine. Instead, he advocated 'learning webs' across which individuals might learn more freely with peers.

Interesting fact: Illich was heavily influenced by Christian thought, though he believed that the Catholic Church had corrupted Christianity. The Church, he thought, presents itself as a kind of insurance company, insuring the believer against the risks of the next life.

> '*I am condemned to be free.*'
> Jean-Paul Sartre

Giving stuff up

For Ivan Illich, our problem is not having *enough* choice but precisely having *too much* choice. He realized that it's not until you commit to something that you actually enjoy it. If there are too many choices, you can spend a whole life flitting from one thing to the next. Perhaps that doesn't much matter when it comes to eating breakfast. But what about people?

Think of an online dating website. Again, it presents you with copious choice, all kinds of possible partners. That can be exhilarating, especially if you've previously wondered whether there is anyone out there for you at all. But it's not actually choice that's the problem. It's commitment. It's only when you meet someone, and give yourself to them, and they to you, that you know the liberation of love. Dating websites may, therefore, lock you into a practice that actually works against your freedom.

Illich's heretical proposal was that, in today's world of plentiful choice, we can find freedom only in giving some of that choice up. He advocated renunciation, and discovering that we can do without. Therein lies a real revelation for modern humanity.

Illich's analysis of the way the modern world constrains us went deeper than just worrying about choice. The problem is much more subtle and interesting than a consumer crisis. We live, Illich recognized, in very paradoxical times. It's true that the state and/or the free market offer guarantees for our security – in the military services, health services, educational services and public services on offer. We pay our taxes and we get to live a life that most of our forebears would have thought extraordinarily blessed. And yet, there's a price we pay for this security, and that price is the loss of a kind of freedom.

For all these services have the effect of incorporating our lives into a series of systems. They are essentially information systems, and they take on a life of their own. By submitting to them, if for the very best of reasons, our lives tend to become shaped by the imperatives of the system, not by our own intentions.

Slave to the system

This sounds strange, though after a little reflection it makes sense. You experience it every time you are kept waiting in a call centre queue and then, when a person answers, they are unable to meet your request because it doesn't fit the workflow. It's a phenomenon that has been popularized in the TV catchphrase 'Computer says no'. You are likely to experience it in the workplace too. Perhaps you spend your days filing reports, keeping to targets, meeting quotas, supplying feedback, not because these things are of much obvious benefit in themselves, but simply because bosses – working for the system – require them.

Another part of modern life that occupied Illich, and compromises our freedom he argued, is the habit of buying insurance. He once commented: 'I cannot let anybody insure the material or the spiritual future for me. I know I live in a world where the greater our ideals are, the greater the insurance companies will become.' The point is that when we try to satisfy all our ideals by buying insurance – from mortgages to pensions

– we lose the possibility that our ideals may be fulfilled in ways that are unexpected to us, that lie ahead of us in the future, that might come to us freely, as gifts. Insurance buys us security, and in that sense is a great good. But it does so at a cost.

The element that is confusing about the world of systems is that it offers us many advantages – those of welfare, education and security. And yet, in so doing, it treats us as abstract objects, not real human beings. We are processed by the system, and thereby risk losing the freedom to be ourselves. Even more so than the choice that hinders, the systems-dominated nature of contemporary life dehumanizes us. We're constrained in the way we relate to others and ourselves.

The freedom of the Good Samaritan

Now, it might be thought that rehumanizing the world could only be a good thing, that regaining the freedom to relate to one another as human beings would be a joy. It can be, Illich says, but it will also be frightening. The issue here is that so much about what is good in human individuals, and that is a

Figure 7
Vincent van Gogh's depiction of *The Good Samaritan* (1890), after a painting by Eugène Delacroix.

delight to experience, stems from the fact that we're suffering creatures too. It's exposure to suffering that the systems world insulates us from.

A brilliant expression of what's at stake here is captured in the story of the Good Samaritan. Illich was gripped by this story because it stresses that the Samaritan who attends to the robbed man lying in the ditch was deeply moved by what he sees – moved in his guts. He attends to the man's needs for sure. But first, he opens himself to a feeling of visceral sympathy.

This is a moment of vulnerability. It is a moment of profound humanity. It's that moment that is lost when we don't take care of others, but absolve ourselves of responsibility and hand their welfare over to systems, in this case that of state health care. The political background to the story expresses the same idea at a different level, when you remember that Samaritans and Jews were supposed to be enemies. The Good Samaritan ignores the politics. He shows how he is free to love the injured Jew outside of the constraints of the nationalistic systems that would otherwise separate them. He is free to care for whomever he wants to. But he causes consternation in those who are trapped by the politics of the day.

How then to be free?

The way to express the kind of human contact Illich argues we should value is captured in the word *conspiratio*. It's the word from which we get 'conspiracy', though the Latin means 'union'. It was what Christians used to do when they shared the kiss of peace during the sharing of the Eucharist. It's free and self-giving, risking even being exposed to the smell of another's breath. That visceral, embodied quality again. It's what we need to know in order to regain the freedom to be human.

Friendship becomes an important part of this freer way of life too, because true friendship operates solely on the basis of what two or more people are to each other as human beings. It's why Illich was so committed to hospitality, as well as study, because the dining table is the locus of friendship. 'What can I in this very moment, in the unique *hic et nunc*, here and now, in which I am, do to get out of this world of needs satisfaction and feel free to hear, to sense, to intuit what the other one wants from me?' he once said.

Making renunciations

So how can we, caught up in these systems, be free? It's not that we want to be rid of them all. That's why freedom is never a straightforward issue.

The practice Illich suggests is renunciation. It's a religious word in origin, a giving up of something because, as it's put in Christianity, the believer lives *in* the world but is not ultimately determined *by* the world. They are waiting for a different kind of world that is to come, one that is truly free. But before that comes about, and partly to bring it on, the individual can anticipate the bigger freedom by enjoying little freedoms – what Illich calls 'little acts of foolish renunciation'. They are foolish because they look silly in a systems world driven by efficiency and choice, though to do so is to practise freedom.

Illich is quite clear that these things are not renounced because they are bad. As we've said, systems bring genuine benefits, like security. It's just that they bring them at a price, perhaps one that has become too costly today, and so they need to be reined back. Rather, we give them up in order to become aware of how attached we are to things that weigh us down, not least choice itself, which can become a burden in the name of being a liberation. In so doing, we'll be surprised by how well we can get along without this and that. Therein lies an experience of freedom. 'The certainty that I can get along without is one of the most efficacious ways of convincing yourself that you are free,' he says.

So self-imposed limits are the basis of practising freedom. Realizing that we can do it is a joy. 'A contemporary practice of renunciation is the opposite of mortification or asceticism or any of the other terms founded upon an ideology of self-denial,' Illich says. 'Rather it is the precondition of enjoyment, for a sober enjoyment of what lies within our reach.' Asceticism is not a bad word in his book; it's not ash-coloured by denial and flagellation. Instead, it is a practice that opens up the now to us, that frees us from hindrances. It lightens the burdens of life so that, no longer stooping, we can raise our eyes to see what's around us. By renunciation we open ourselves to gratuity; the spirit of receiving a gift.

What these renunciations also deliver alongside freedom is hope. With them, we are exposed once more to the kindness of strangers, the people we don't know who nonetheless show us friendship. To put it another way, if we stop relying just on systems, and sometimes turn to our fellows, we discover that humanity is good. It's a liberation.

A Step

Here are three 'foolish renunciations' you might like to try:

1 Don't eat meat, perhaps on a Friday, not because you fear for the suffering of animals (though you might), but because restricting your diet might mean you enjoy food more.

2 Don't write emails but write letters, for the very reason that it takes more time, time that you are giving to another person.

3 Don't take a flight, or do one trip not by car, not because you'll reduce your carbon footprint, but because you'll open yourself to new experiences brought through travelling by train or walking.

8

Friendship – its perils and promise

Few would doubt that friendship is key to life; indeed it might well be thought the heart of a good life. You might have every good thing that life can offer, but if you don't have any friends then all those things would lose their lustre. The reason is, in a way, simple: we are social animals. We need to be with others. We find ourselves only with others. Loneliness is not just painful; it can lead to insanity, even death.

But what is friendship? What is this relationship that is so crucial to us? What are its nature, its rules, its perils, its promise? Can colleagues be friends, can online strangers, can lovers? Is friendship a kind of love? What is the defining feature of the love that we call friendship? These are the questions we must pursue.

> 'Friends have all things in common.'
> Plato

Aristotle's classification

The ancient Greek philosophers spent a lot of time trying to define friendship, to work out precisely what it is. The problem is that so many different kinds of relationship can be called friendly or seem like a variety of friendship. You might call everyone from your best friend and partner to your hairdresser or the guy you meet at the gym 'a friend'. What can these relationships be said to hold in common?

Aristotle had a good idea. He thought that any relationship which involves a mutual exchange of goodwill can be called friendly. If you wish someone well, and they wish you well, then they are in a sense your friend. But of course that is not enough. So he took things a step further. He believed that there are three types of friendship. His classification is enormously useful when it comes to thinking about the friends you have.

Aristotle (384–322 bce)

Quick summary: Aristotle learned his philosophy from Plato, though after 20 years at Plato's Academy he set up his own 'school' in Athens, the Lyceum. He is remembered today also for his study of logic, the categorization of plants and animals, and politics.

Key text: His ideas on friendship can be found in the *Nicomachean Ethics*, Books VIII and IX. The *Nicomachean Ethics* is really a set of lecture notes, and so reads as rather jumbled, but it is full of resonant ideas.

Interesting fact: Aristotle was the tutor to Alexander the Great.

Three types of friend

1 The first group are friends primarily because they are useful to each other – like an employee and a boss, or a doctor and a patient, or a politician and an ally; they share goodwill because they get something out of the relationship. They do not love each other for themselves but only insofar as there is some good that they get from each other, Aristotle observes. They do not even have to be particularly nice people for a certain kind of friendship to thrive. This kind of friendship therefore lasts only as long as the useful thing it is based on continues to be exchanged. This is why, for example, if

you change jobs, nine times out of ten the friendships you shared at work will not continue. The useful thing that underpinned the friendship – work – has stopped. So does the friendship.

2   The second group are friends primarily because some pleasure is enjoyed by being with them; it may be football, shopping, gossip or physical intimacy, but the friendship thrives insofar, and probably only insofar, as the thing that gives the pleasure continues to exist between them. Aristotle noted that young people are especially enamoured with this sort of friendship – since the young live by emotion and more than anything else pursue what is pleasant to them. If

pleasures are quick to change and fall away, so too are these friendships.

One case in point is the friendship that arises from an infatuation. For as long as the passion lasts, the young lovers feel like they have the best friend in the world. But that kind of love can stop as quickly as it started, and with its coming and going comes and goes the friendship. When the pleasure found in the other ceases, the friendship fades too.

3 The third group is people who love each other for who they are in themselves. It may be their depth of character, their innate goodness, their intensity of passion or their simple *joie de vivre*, but once established on such a basis these friendships are ones that last. Undoubtedly much will be given and much taken too, but the friendship itself is independent of external factors and immensely more valuable than the friendships that fall into the first two groups. The better these friends are as people, the better the quality of the friendship. This friendship is therefore also the rarest. And it takes time to grow: they must 'savour salt' together, Aristotle says – by which he meant both that good friends must eat together, and share some 'salty' life experiences. It is only then the profound bonds of trust, characteristic of this love, become strong.

That there are better or higher friendships – we call them soul-mates, close or old friends, or best friends – as opposed to more casual friendships or mere friendliness, is surely right.

Aristotle noted that the first two groups are therefore like each other because, if you take the utility or the pleasure away, then the chances are the friendship will fade. This, though, is not true of the third group.

What is friendship?

Clearly, friendliness can be part of all kinds of relationship. Moreover, most people want to be friends with their partner, with a work colleague or two, and even with members of their family. But if friendship has no clear boundaries, can we say anything about its chief characteristic?

How about this: if the love shared in families has much to do with wanting to *care* for others, and the love shared by lovers is primarily one that longs to *have* another, then maybe the love shared by friends is one that along with everything else longs to *know* another, and be known by them.

For example, ask yourself what a characteristic activity of friends might be? One idea would be that friends talk. The act of talking, face-to-face, is the way that friends get to know each other better. Alternatively, when good friends have been apart, they say things like, 'We picked up just where we left off: it's as if we had never stopped talking.' These friends know each other and like nothing better than to chat on the phone or text.

Other qualities matter too, like loyalty and trust, along with factors such as simply making an effort and time for your friends. Put all this together, and you have the content of friendship. That's what it looks like.

> 'An honest answer is the sign of true friendship.'
> Proverbs 24:26

Another self

Aristotle had another way of defining friends. A friend, he said, is 'another self'. Today, we might take this to mean that a close friend is a mirror of your own self, someone with whom you find personal resonances, thereby realizing that, though autonomous, you are not alone; there is someone quite like you and whom you quite like.

But for Aristotle something more connected, more dependent is being described too. The sense of being another self for two friends is that, in a sense, they are one. Like two eyes gazing at the world, their operation is conjoined. I do not find out who I am in solipsistic, narcissistic isolation, but I do so in my friendships. I can no more be a full person without a friend than a magnet can exist as a single pole. Perhaps we still hear an echo of this when we say of a friend, 'I basked in her reflected glory.' I have done nothing; but it is as if her doing were mine too.

Online friendship

It's worth throwing a new experience of friendship into this mix, since it's become very common. To do so, consider this story.

A friend of mine went to meet a stranger. Only, this person wasn't really a stranger at all. The two had already spent hours together on a social networking site. Judging by her messages, picture and blog, my friend felt confident that she would be likeable, perhaps even lovable. Yet he was also anxious and unsure.

Meeting someone face-to-face has taken on a new meaning with the advent of social networking sites. In a reversal of normal experience, meeting someone is increasingly happening *after* getting to know them. But do you really *know* them? Therein lies the frisson and fear.

Part of the problem with this sort of encounter is that, well, screens *screen*. That is to say, no matter how authentic it may feel, communication over the internet is carried out, for the most part, blind and deaf. When reading an instant message or a personal blog, we can neither see the author nor hear them.

In other words, if the silicon universe is not to leave one as lonely as Major Tom, it may be necessary to realize that the context for real friendship is not within this infinite, shapeless medium but rather in the close intimacy of embodied exchange. We can of course be *friendly* online. Like chatting in the corner shop or smiling on the bus, courtesy makes on- and off-line worlds infinitely better places. Nevertheless, there is as big a gap between *friendliness* and *friendship* as there is between co-operation and love; we forget the difference at our peril.

It may well be that today we have wider circles of friends because of the internet. And that might be a boon. But beware: there is nothing more ruinous of relationships than thinking they are something they are not. And friendship may be particularly prone to such blind spots, as friendship per se is something people rarely think about.

A Step

It is striking that, while most people would say they value their friends far more than they value money, they nonetheless spend much more time earning money than they do nurturing their friendships. So, try spending some time cultivating a friendship. Even a fraction of the time that you spend at work, spent on friends, might make a vast difference.

Don't just put a note up on Facebook; pick up the phone and make a call. Offer to do something with a friend that you might usually only do with family, like going on holiday or spending Christmas together. Make a rule that you will see your closest friends at least once a week, or month. Friendship is probably more important than anything else in life, as Aristotle averred. You can be guaranteed a return on your amity investment.

9

Gratitude – and the surprise called life

WHY *are children taught to say thank you? When you think about it, the answer is not that clear. Is it the politeness that makes Mummy happy, when Timmy murmured words of gratitude, quite unprompted, as Grandpa topped up his pocket money last week?*

Most parents would think that Timmy did the right thing. But perhaps he did not. Perhaps, secretly, he thought that Grandpa was only doing what a decent grandpa should. Grandpa, in turn, might have preferred *not* to be thanked at all. Being thanked, after all, denies Grandpa the chance of giving out of sheer gratuity. Then again, Timmy might have said nothing in order to recognize Grandpa's endearing modesty. He'd be honouring Grandpa in his silence.

Or did Grandpa actually give to have his gift acknowledged, and for the selfish pleasure it would give him to have his grandson salute the generosity? Parents frequently tell their children off for not saying thank you. But how many grown ups give to children manipulatively, making a show of their largesse in order to win love? They want to hear that thank you. They're upset when they don't.

*'My children are ungrateful: they don't care.
That is my great reward. They are free.'*
Fay Weldon

Simone Weil

(1909–43)

Quick summary: Weil was a French philosopher and mystic whose aphoristic writings attempt to penetrate to the unexpected nature of things, an exercise that she called 'extreme attention'.

Key text: *Simone Weil: An Anthology* is a book to read slowly; you need to sink into her thought.

Interesting fact: A brilliant student, she then worked alongside the poor in a car factory, fought in the Spanish Civil War, and died at the age of 34.

Changing reality

Weil wrote in order to redress balances. She believed she should analyse various facets of life, like work and love, and so highlight the values in them she believed the modern world overlooked. 'If we know in what way society is unbalanced, we must do what we can to add weight to the lighter scale,' she wrote. The familiar might thereby become strange again. It would have the advantage of helping us escape what she referred

Figure 9 Portrait of Simone Weil.

to as the deadening 'gravity' of routine ways of thinking, and so be open to the extraordinary giftedness of life, what she called the lightness of 'grace'. Gravity is that which drags us down. Grace, though, raises us up.

Her thoughts on gratitude are useful as it is a virtue over which we have lost this sense of surprise. We've lost it, not just because parents drum those two short words 'thank you' into our little heads; gratitude has also suffered as a result of the recent trend that links it to human happiness. This is the teaching that saying thank you will make you happy. Psychologists of happiness recommend practices like jotting in a notebook – a 'gratitude diary' – at least five things each day for which you are glad. It doesn't matter what. A tasty sandwich at lunchtime. An affectionate wave from the wife. The belief is that being aware of what's good, and taking a moment to be thankful for it, gives you something, a kind of kick. It has been shown to boost the levels of happy hormones inside your head.

Quite as effectively as parental chiding, this practice destroys true gratitude by the manner in which it attempts to nurture it. One advocate notes: 'To express thankfulness is to attract goodness.' Another enthuses: 'We can actually change our reality by being grateful first.' It's an instrumental approach that undermines the link between gratitude, grace and gratuity. As William Faulkner observed: 'Maybe the only thing worse than having to give gratitude constantly all the time, is having to accept it.'

The fact is that true gratitude arises because you *are* grateful. It's spontaneous, not contrived. If you don't feel grateful for life, and so rarely say thank you, then any supposedly thankful words uttered will be as empty as little Timmy's, who only speaks them to avoid a clip around the head. There is no reverse-engineering gratitude into existence. It's the awareness that life is pure gift which must come first. And it's by her 'extreme attention' that Weil can help us with that – the nub of the issue.

Exiting and existence

Weil's writings offered meditations on a number of elements that contribute to true gratitude. And it's worth noting that her thoughts have little to do with happiness. In fact, she recommended a strict indifference to that which makes you happy, as it's promise is, as often as not, a false one. What matters in life is that which is good, and that which is good might well lead to sadness. For example, love is good and 'love on the part of someone who is happy is the wish to share the suffering of the beloved who is unhappy,' she commented. That's a fact which any parent knows to be true: they can simultaneously feel grateful and anxious for their child. They might, on occasion, be most conscious of that gratitude when they feel most anxious about the child.

So gratitude comes from existence. And what is existence? Weil asks. The word itself is quite similar to the word *exit*. If *exit* means 'to go outside', *exist* means 'to be placed outside'. So one shows gratitude to that which one comes out of, for one's existence. It might be a parent, it might be nature, or it might be God.

Thank what?

Here's something else to note. The verb *to thank* is transitive. It needs an object. In specific cases – for instance 'Thanks, Mum, for cooking chips' – that's fine. But in the most generalized 'thanks for life' sense – 'the how wonderful life is while you're in the world' sense – to whom is the thanks directed? It can't be you yourself, because no matter how wonderful you are, you are not the author of your own existence. You came out of elsewhere. Similarly, the gratitude here seems to be suggesting more than just that I want to thank Mum. And if I do, next time I see her, she might well pass on most of the responsibility to others involved, like dad.

Is the gratitude directed at an indifferent universe, assuming for the moment that it's not directed at a creator?

Perhaps gratitude towards evolutionary processes? That doesn't make much sense, as they are blind. Or perhaps the sense is not directed at anyone or thing, but rather the gratitude reflects an appreciation of the luck that your life and mine is simply given; the thanks is for the brute fact of it. No more, no less.

This, perhaps surprisingly, is quite close to the kind of Christian insight Simone Weil espoused. It affirms the doctrine of creation *ex nihilo* (out of nothing), which stresses too that life is simply given: our creation comes literally and dizzyingly out of nothing – no reason, no conspiracy, no purpose, no previously existing quantum field from which matter might have spontaneously emerged. 'Creation is an act of love and it is perpetual,' Weil wrote. Strictly speaking, it's pointless. So why should there be gratitude?

The reason is that there is a difference between an atheistic givenness and the theistic version. In the latter, creation, which is simply a given, is still actively made. But it is made in a sense that is entirely beyond us. All our uses of the word *made* must be *from* something or *for* something. Creation, though, is not 'made' from or for or out of anything, according to the *ex nihilo* doctrine. We're pushing at the limits of understanding here, which is one of the reasons that Weil qualified her attention to things with the word *extreme*. The idea that the *ex nihilo* doctrine points to is the gratuitousness of creation. All 13.7 billion years of it made. . . just because, simply given.

To put it another way, our creation is pure, sheer and utter donation; it is radically gifted. As gift, it is given, for the believer, not by an indifferent universe – which being indifferent can't give anything anyway – but by the mystery referred to as God. It comes out of God's will, and that is the reason a believer is thankful. It's why gratitude is closely linked to wonder. The believer can affirm with the atheist that life is simply given – no strings attached, not for anything – though rather than just being grateful for the luck of it, he or she is simultaneously grateful to God.

I should perhaps add that I speak here as an agnostic. What's striking, I think, is that where the atheist gratitude must admit a certain limited quality (not entirely unlike being grateful that your numbers came up at the bingo), the believer affirms the quality of a profound mystery. Perhaps that's why gratitude has become a bit of a problem in the Western world, unsure about deities, and so we need psychologists to persuade us to show it.

> *'In most of mankind gratitude is merely a secret hope for greater favours.'*
> La Rochefoucauld

Given to give away

Whatever you make of God, there's something else that is worth contemplating too. For, if my life itself is a gift, it cannot, strictly speaking, be given to me. That would assume I was around to be given the gift of life that made me be around. But I am not, until the gift is given, so I cannot already be around to receive it. This is not mere sophistry. It's part of the attempt to make gratitude surprising again. What it implies is that life that is radically gifted must be given on, and on, and on. It can't stop. If you come to a point where you truly see that life is a gift, something that I presume only saints manage, it can no more be held on to than a flame can hold on to the light it emits once lit.

This brings us to a definition of what it is to be grateful. It is to share that which you received as a gift. (It also suggests a definition of ingratitude, giving something and expecting it back with more besides. Ingratitude, then, has another name: debt. The opposite of gift is something like lending a loan on interest. It explains why we can never really feel grateful to our bank manager.)

Such a definition of gratitude explains why the rich man in the story will find it harder to get to heaven than a camel will to make it through the eye of a needle. The rich man who hoards his possessions is not grateful for what he has, because if he understood the nature of wealth aright he would share it around – gifting what he received. It's not that there's anything wrong with wealth per se. Rather, what's wrong is not seeing that giving is the only act of gratitude worthy of the name. You could go so far as to think that merely saying thank you for what you've got is to do the opposite: to lay claim to it. It's precisely not to recognize that what you've got always rests on an initial gift, the gift of life itself. So you should really share it.

Incidentally, this is not just a Christian insight. In the Hindu tradition there is a similar teaching. There is a period of life, it says, when it is appropriate to gather and gain. But that period should be followed by another when you give what you have gained away. It might be a financial gifting, or of talent, expertise or time. That is what it is to be truly grateful. Giving in gratitude comes about because of the realization that everything is grace, everything is given, is gift.

So true gratitude comes about not because it's polite to say thank you, as a parent teaches a child. Neither does it come about because you hope to get something back, like happiness. It comes out of the recognition that what you have comes out of nothing. Gratitude is the recognition that life is pure gift.

Practising gratitude must, therefore, be done indirectly. If it rests on a sense of the giftedness of existence, then giving gratuitously would be one way of reminding yourself of that. Tithing is the religious observation; charity the secular version, though Weil thinks it must be indiscriminate in order to be a proper practice of gratitude. That's because, for her, God's creativity is also indiscriminate. It's just given. Try 'just giving' too.

10

Hope – and the courage to be

WE all have hope for the future, or at least anyone who believes life is worth living has hope. Those who don't, and despair, also despair for life, which is why the existentialist writer Albert Camus put hope at the top of the agenda, when he noted that, 'There is but one truly serious philosophical problem, and that is suicide' – the one truly hopeless act. And yet, for so serious a matter, the nature of hope is rarely explored in depth, and is also routinely mocked. 'What is hope?' asked Lord Byron. 'Nothing but the paint on the face of existence.'

The serious problem is how to nurture hope in a way that is neither wildly optimistic, cultivating the deluded power of positive thinking; nor wildly cynical, so as to avoid being caught up in perpetual cycles of despair. Have hope! It can be got right.

'While there's life there's hope.'
English proverb

Thomas Aquinas (1224–74)

Quick summary: The greatest of the medieval theologians,
Aquinas is also listed as among the greatest moral philosophers
of all time. His achievement was to introduce the Western
world to Aristotle once more, after the ancient Greek's works
reappeared from the East. He did much more than that,
however, deepening Aristotle's insights greatly, especially with
regard to the virtues and emotions.

Key text: His writing can be difficult as it is too logical and dry for
modern tastes. I can recommend Herbert McCabe's *On Aquinas*
(2008) for a warm and witty introduction.

Interesting fact: Aquinas became a Dominican monk, a move
that shocked his aristocratic family. The story goes that two
of his brothers locked him in a tower, and supplied him with
a voluptuous woman, in an attempt to dissuade him. It didn't
work.

The work of hope

Aquinas would have agreed with Camus that hope is of
critical importance in any life that can be called good, though
for different reasons: along with faith and love, hope is one of
the cardinal virtues celebrated by Christianity. That said, one
thing immediately strikes you about his account of it. Hope is
arduous.

Hope is hard work because it's concerned with what we
don't have. The more distant what we desire is, the greater the
need for hope. It's what the imprisoned hostage must hold on
to, day after day in the dark cell. It's for individuals who don't
shy from reality, but can stare reality in the face.

The novelist J. G. Ballard had it, when his wife died too
young and suddenly, after what should have been a routine
operation to have her appendix removed. 'From the start,'
Ballard writes, 'I was determined to keep my family together.'
Notice he uses the word *start* determinedly. That's the

courageous virtue called hope. He continues: 'Many people (who should have known better) openly told me that a mother's loss was irreplaceable and the children would be affected for ever.' He did not submit to their hopelessness for one moment.

Another characteristic of hopefulness is that it is not rosy. 'Alcohol was a close friend and confident in the early days,' he confesses. And yet, his hope was firm. 'I loved my children deeply, as they knew.' Hope is informed by a realism that can cope with the worst and yearn for better.

The hopeful mindset

There are two kinds of hope, according to Aquinas, though they are related. The first kind is an emotion, a sort of passion or exhilaration. It's the feeling we have when we long for something that is pleasurable, but difficult. The balloonist says

Figure 10 *The Seven Virtues – Hope* (1561/2), engraving by Pieter Bruegel the Elder. Hope at work in a dangerous world. The Latin motto at the bottom reads *The assurance that hope gives us is most pleasant and most essential to an existence amid so many nearly unsupportable woes.*

she hopes to fly over Everest and beat the world record, as she grins, draws in breath, and marshals her fibre for the task. The hope is fulfilled when the day is clear, the balloon catches the jet stream, and she sails across the heavens at over 30,000 feet.

The second kind of hope is cognitive, a habit of mind. It's the commitment we make to a belief or cause in which we place our hope. Again, what we hope for will be difficult to achieve. If it weren't difficult we wouldn't have to hope for it, but would merely look forward to it. This kind of hope delivers confidence and courage. Without it, the mind is filled with despair or fear. The politician has this kind of hope when she presents her programme for the country, believing it will make the nation a better place.

The emotion of hope, and the hopeful mindset, are related because our feelings are related to our beliefs. A good politician conveys hope not just by explaining *why* their programme will lead to the common good but also by *inspiring* us, often using exhilarating rhetoric. Hope becomes infectious when it combines the two qualities. One is needed to check the other, too. Pure emotion alone might hope for something that is ridiculously beyond reach; the purely intellectual belief will find it hard to sustain the confidence and courage that are required to realize its greatest hopes.

An active passion

Hope is different from optimism, because optimism doesn't demand much from us, whereas hope is always a challenge. Strictly speaking, we should say, 'I'm optimistic it won't rain tomorrow,' rather than, 'I hope it won't rain tomorrow.' Optimism is passive; there's nothing we can do about the weather. Similarly, an optimistic person is not inspiring as a person of hope is: optimism is little more than a fluke of character or perhaps a product of having the right hormones. Optimism may well be entirely deluded too.

A person of hope, though, conveys a belief and strength that may well be against the odds. Hope can bring out the best in us and can even make what was unlikely more likely. Hope has a reflexive quality that tends to increase the odds. Hope against hope tests impossibilities. The Czech playwright and politician Václav Havel understood this when he wrote: 'Hope is definitely not the same thing as optimism. It is not the conviction that something will turn out well, but the certainty that something makes sense, regardless of how it turns out.' Hope is an active focus on the good that can change the world.

Still, hope keeps a firm eye on the real world. If it is not optimistic, it is not utopian either. A moral hero, such as the South African cleric Desmond Tutu, embodies this balance. He has seen the horrors of poverty. 'I must admit that I was quite overwhelmed by what I saw in the teeming slums of Calcutta and Madras,' he writes in an essay called 'My Credo'. 'I was truly devastated by what I had experienced.' And then he lived under the obscenity of apartheid. 'The world was in a horrendous mess.' But he can hold on to hope because he has also experienced 'the indomitable resilience of the human spirit, which did not seem to know that it was unequal to the struggle and should by rights have long ago thrown in the towel'.

> *'Hope without an object cannot live.'*
> Samuel Taylor Coleridge

Good hope

Hope also has a moral character, according to Aquinas, which is what makes it a very great virtue. We hope for what is good, the good thing we hope for being what inspires hope in us, along with the commitment it demands. 'I hope that my son will survive the surgery,' confesses a mum as she gears herself up for the wait. 'Our hope is that one day poverty will be eradicated,' proclaims the director of a charity, as she and her fellow workers muster up the strength to keep up the good work. The greater the good hoped for, the greater the hope placed in it.

But is that right? There is an immediate objection to deal

with here – the observation that hope is not always moral, because people hope for bad things too. The murderer, for instance, hopes he will get away with his crime. One could retort that the murderer is still hoping for what's good, only in this particular case, it's what's good for him, not what's good in itself. But that would be sophistry, and it would also miss the deeper reason hope must be for what's good, and not just in the sense of 'what's good for me'. This is because to hope for what's not good is self-defeating, sooner or later. According to Aquinas, only what is truly good can sustain the hope of its coming, in the long term. To hope for what's bad defeats hope: the emotion turns to despair, the habit of mind to cynicism.

You see this conveyed in the TV series *The Wire*. On first viewing, it is a drama about Baltimore cops and drug dealers. The good cops hope to catch the bad dealers. The dealers, for their part, hope to stay in business. But soon you realize that hope has nothing to do with it. Cops and dealers alike are instead caught in what is referred to as 'the game'. There's no right or wrong on the housing estates of Baltimore, just moves. The police make a move, and the dealers respond. The dealers make a move, and the police fight back. It becomes hard to tell the good and bad guys apart. There is no hope in the game, and the game won't release you. Dealers with hope for the future, and who try to leave the game, are invariably shot. Police who leave become losers. Hope is driven out. This is what 'hoping' for what's not good achieves.

Grounds for hope

Back to the notion that the greater the good, the greater the hope, because for Aquinas, there is a critical corollary that follows. There is no greater good, or hope, than God. He argues that God is not only a good thing to hope for, but that God is the only thing truly worthy of human hope. This is because only God can provide the good things that we most dearly need. When hope is placed in God, hope can never be thwarted. 'All my hope on God is founded,' wrote the hymn writer.

For the believer, this will make eminent sense. Even for the unsure, or disbelieving, there is a valuable insight to be gleaned from Aquinas's assertion, no less. It is the link between hope and faith.

Faith here means trust, not the assertion of metaphysical convictions. Aquinas trusts in God. He would never have trusted in the tooth fairy or the Flying Spaghetti Monster, even if such creatures existed. It's this kind of faith, or trust, that is an integral part of the dynamic of hope. To put it the other way, a good question to ask yourself is whether you can trust what you base your hope upon. If you can, you can conclude that your hope is well founded. If not, you might need to think again.

People trust in many things. Some trust in science, a good choice if you're hoping to understanding the nature of dark matter; not such a good choice if you're hoping for an end to all wars. There are those that place their trust in family life, hoping that it will provide them with the fulfilment that, say, they don't find at work. It's a reasonable choice, families being a great source of fulfilment for many people, though not one without its risks, as families are also a great source of distress.

Others again, perhaps running from their families, will turn to work, hoping that it delivers what they seek from life; money in their pocket, a sense of achievement. These are good things. And work may be worthy of your trust; it partly makes sense to place your hope in it. But like family, work can let you down, when your boss is overbearing or the boom turns to bust.

Aquinas would whisper in your ear that it is precisely because other sources of hope are unreliable that God is the only real source of hope. We are made for God, he says, 'and so the proper and principle object of hope is indeed eternal blessedness.'

You, like me, may not be able to share in that faith entirely, or perhaps only on days when you feel hopeful. But the underlying challenge is a powerful one: in what do you place your faith? If you seek to have real hope in your life – the kind that is courageous, realistic and makes possible what seemed impossible – it's a question that needs to be asked.

11

Humour – its humanity and humility

HUMOUR *is clearly part of the good life. It's highly pleasurable for one thing, and for another, enterprising psychologists somewhere have surely shown that frequency of laughter is directly correlated to reduced heart disease, or some such. Happy people laugh, as do those who approach life cheerfully and attentively. The witty have wits. And that's good.*

But there's more to humour than light relief and health benefits. Its value as a virtue is not instrumental. It's what humour reveals to us about the limits of human understanding or, to put it another way, humour has much to do with humility. In fact, a good laugh is certainly the most enjoyable and least pretentious way of exercising that otherwise tricky virtue: modesty. It's got to be humour of the best kind, of course – free of contempt, sarcasm and prejudice. But there's something rather wonderful in this quintessentially human activity. The human, humour and humility are profoundly linked.

> *'I love such mirth as does not make friends
> ashamed to look upon one another next
> morning.'*
> Izaak Walton

Arthur Schopenhauer (1788–1860)

Quick guide: The irony of turning to Schopenhauer for guidance on humour is that he is famous as a pessimist. Even his mother disliked him because of his thoroughly gloomy looks.

Key text: *The World as Will and Representation* is his magnum opus. It's broken into neat sections that make it more accessible. He also wrote essays and aphorisms.

Interesting fact: He was the first Western philosopher in modern times to engage with Eastern philosophy, particularly as found in the Hindu scriptures the Upanishads.

Why's that funny?

According to Schopenhauer, the source of humour – or the ludicrous, as he calls it – is paradox. We see something in an incongruous situation, and that's what makes us laugh. The greater the inappropriateness of the object out of context, the greater the surprise, the more violent the laughter. Schopenhauer kindly supplies his readers with examples.

There is the inappropriate epitaph of the physician who has died: 'Here like a hero he lies, and those he has slain lie around him.' There's the ridiculous logic of the Austrian who liked to walk in the mountains alone. One day he came by another walker who confessed to the same pleasure. 'Well, let us walk together,' he suggested. Or the comment made by Mercutio, in Shakespeare's *Romeo and Juliet*, who mortally wounded, remarks: 'Ask for me tomorrow, and you shall find me a grave man.'

As further examples, Schopenhauer tells the story of the two proudest lions in the zoo, who one night broke through the bars that separated them. So fierce was their fight, so uncontrolled their rage, that they devoured each other, and in the morning nothing was left of either but their tails. Or there is the story of the poor man, whom a king saw trembling with cold on account of it being winter. 'Return to your wardrobe and put on more clothes', the king advised, thinking of his own copious closet. 'I follow your advice already, my Lord, and to the letter,' the serf humbly replied: 'Your servant wears his entire wardrobe.'

Schopenhauer argues that the reason certain animals, like apes and kangaroos, can appear ludicrous to us is because we see something human in them – perhaps a glance in their eyes, or the manner in which they tend their young – and that sits incongruously alongside their other behaviours, be it the gibbering chatter of the ape or the bounding leap of the kangaroo.

In all these cases, the source of the humour is the unexpected juxtaposition of certain objects, ideas or words. And I think Schopenhauer is right: if you put to one side the humour that is based upon contempt, the entertainingly inappropriate is

There was an Old Lady whose folly
Induced her to sit in a holly;
Whereon, by a thorn her dress being torn,
She quickly became melancholy.

Figure 11 Edward Lear was a master of the absurd, as depicted in this cartoon from *A Book of Nonsense* (1846).

a good hypothesis for the huge diversity of things that we laugh at. But what of its moral significance?

The serious character

The moral character of humour becomes clearer when you think of the opposite of wit and jokes: seriousness. A serious mood sets in when there is no paradox or irony. 'The serious person is convinced', Schopenhauer writes, 'that he conceives things as they are, and that they are as he conceives them.' Such individuals are sure they are right. They are blinkered, unable to conceive of anything that might fall outside their ability to comprehend it. They live in a world in which they can account for everything, smoothly and coherently. Nothing takes them by surprise. Nothing provokes laughter. To put it another way, seriousness is the opposite of humility, because the serious person is hubristic. They know it all. They've seen it all before.

Similarly, the serious person hates to be laughed at. It offends them so easily because it challenges so effectively their self-importance. For them being made to look ridiculous or ludicrous is one of the worst kinds of insult.

The humour advantage

That seriousness is the opposite of humour explains why the switch from profound seriousness to laughter is particularly funny, and often comes about unawares. The double entendre, the unintended comment. Such things prick bubbles. It's why individuals who can use humour to lighten moods are so appealing to us. At one level, they make us laugh, and so offer us a moment of pleasure. But at another level, they imply that they have the more attractive, humble character. Thus, the politician who is relentlessly serious suffers from a serious disadvantage.

The other context in which humour is a great blessing is in matters of love. Again, the reason is that love is simultaneously both serious and ridiculous. Witness the actions of lovers. Love is, Schopenhauer explains:

'the cause of war and the aim and object of peace, the basis of the series and the aim of the joke, the inexhaustible source of wit, the key to all hints and allusions. . . it is the daily thought and desire of the young and often of the old as well, the hourly thought of the unchaste, and the constantly recurring reverie of the chaste even against their will, the ever ready material for a joke, only because the profoundest seriousness lies at its root'.

That said, there's a warning here for people who do nothing but make jokes, too. The risk the relentlessly witty face is of appearing never to be serious. Instead, they come across as affected and trivial. If we never have a sense of the real person behind the ludicrousness, we suspect that they might be masking a character flaw, and that undermines the moral worth of humour.

> *'A dirty joke is a sort of mental rebellion.'*
> George Orwell

The highest form of wit

If sarcasm is the lowest form of wit, then the highest is that which is simultaneously quite serious. It's called irony, and what characterizes it is the seamless move from the humorous to the serious, and from the serious to the humorous. Both dimensions are experienced simultaneously.

This is the kind of humour often deployed by the best moralists. Jesus was, apparently, a past master. 'It is easier for a camel to go through the eye of a needle than for the rich man to enter the kingdom of God.' It is amusing now, and must have provoked belly-laughs when the grunting, behumped animals were actually standing close by. There's the moral philosopher David Hume's reflection on human nature: 'It is not contrary to reason to prefer the destruction of the whole world to the scratching of my finger.' Or there's Ghandi's remark on being asked what he thought of modern civilization. 'That would be a very good idea,' he said. Such remarks are amusing and alarming in equal measure.

High wit is also the skill of the clown, the genius of the jester, which perhaps helps explain the tradition to be found in many religions of prophets who are known as 'fools of God'.

In spite of his pessimistic reputation, or perhaps because that reputation is deserved, Schopenhauer was himself more than capable of this deep form of humour. It comes across in some of his aphorisms:

- 'Many undoubtedly owe their good fortune to the circumstance that they possess a pleasing smile with which they win hearts.'
- 'Money is human happiness in abstract; consequently he who is no longer capable of happiness in life sets his whole heart on money.'
- 'Every parting is a foretaste of death, and every reunion a foretaste of resurrection. That is why even people who were indifferent to one another rejoice so much when they meet again after twenty or thirty years.'
- 'If your abilities are only mediocre, modesty is mere honesty; but if you possess great talents, it is hypocrisy.'

Sublime jokes

There's one final dimension to add. If humour's midwife is humility, and humility is an acknowledgement of ignorance, then humour also has much to do with what Schopenhauer calls the *sublime*. The sublime is that which is simultaneously terrible and delightful. It is nature 'in turbulent and tempestuous motion'. It's experiences that remind us of 'vanishing nothingness', such as the sense of falling beneath the night sky or being vanquished by the infinity of a cathedral dome. It's being reminded that our existence is a matter of indifference to, say, the moon which 'without any reference to us. . . moves along eternally foreign to earthly life and activity'.

The thing about the sublime is that it shares the same incongruous logic of the humorous. It's both terrible and delightful. Two opposing sensations are locked together in the experience. Hence people can laugh when faced with something terrible, or conversely cry at the delightful. It's as if our emotional repertoire collapses underneath the weight of the sublime, much as laughter starts when words cease to be an adequate vehicle for what we are feeling in that moment. You've got 'to get' the joke. To explain it, is to explain it away. The sublime is the same.

Another quality that they both share is being satisfying. There is nothing more cathartic than a good laugh, nothing more invigorating than the sublime – particularly when they deliver a sense of the bitter-sweet nature of life. The satisfaction comes, therefore, because life is indeed often bitter-sweet. It's an amalgam of joy and fear, pleasure and pain, hopefulness and despair. Humour and the sublime alike confirm in us that these contradictions are OK. We find consolation.

A Step

There's a very practical tip that comes out of Schopenhauer's analysis. If you want to improve your ability to tell jokes, tell jokes against yourself. Be humbled by your own tongue. It's sure to make others laugh. As someone with male pattern baldness, the hair that remains being ginger, and a penchant for corduroy jackets and trousers, I can tell you: it works. Whether or not self-deprecation makes you humble is not, though, for you yourself to say. Others must be the judge of that, for to declare yourself humble, is in as bad taste as laughing at your own jokes.

12

Individuality – not individualism

THE story of humanity rocks like a pendulum. As the bob of history swings one way, the individual gets lost in the collective. It was this extreme that communist countries, such as China and the Soviet Union, reached during the twentieth century. But as the bob swings the other way, human connectedness and dependency becomes lost in a deepening culture of individualism. It is this excess that may presently characterize life in the West, a place in which politicians have been known to declare there is no such thing as society. When the bob is too far away from its equilibrium position, life becomes crude and brutal – 'red in tooth and claw', as Tennyson said of nature.

But if that's true, people in the West need to be wary of not swinging to the opposite extreme, on the rebound. After all, if selfishness is a vice, and self-sufficiency a delusion, that does not mean that self-esteem and self-knowledge are bad, and that a certain regard for one's self-interests should be condemned either. It's a question of balance – the balance that can be called not individualism, but individuality.

> 'I am large. I contain multitudes.'
> Walt Whitman

Oscar Wilde (1854–1900)

Quick summary: Wilde is known as a playwright and wit, of course, but he is also an important moral philosopher, writing about issues such as integrity, individualism, sexuality and socialism.

Key text: His essays are good, particularly *De Profundis* and *The Soul of Man under Socialism*.

Interesting fact: Wilde has even been recognized by the Vatican as a thinker, the head of protocol in the Catholic city-state having published a book of his sayings.

Style to character

Wilde is remembered for his aestheticism, the great effort of the individual who attempts to make an artwork of his or her own life. (And if you can't be a work of art, you should at least wear one, he remarked.) His credo finds supreme expression in his plays, in which his characters, like those of Shakespeare, speak in a highly stylized form and yet seem all the more human for doing so:

- 'We are all in the gutter, but some of us are looking at the stars.'
- 'Experience is the name every one gives to their mistakes.'
- 'A man who knows the price of everything and the value of nothing.'

Who could utter such phrases in real life without sounding ridiculously pretentious, and yet his characters do so in *Lady Windermere's Fan*, and are never more alive.

What Wilde believed was that the individual, to be him- or herself, must have a deep knowledge of others – other people and times that bear upon their own place and person. No doubt, he was awakened to this imperative as an outsider himself: the Irishman in aristocratic London, concealing his same-sex desires. Being an outsider is to be conscious of your relationships with others, and to be aware of how your own sense of self is intimately caught up with their sense of you. Paradoxically, the outsider who appears to be a model of supreme self-sustained independence, as Wilde surely did, is only so because they are acutely sensitive of others. Wilde could not have written such exquisite plays, with their sharply defined characters, had he not had this highly developed capacity.

Being an insider also leaves you with a keen sense of the complacencies of your times, its ignorance and delusions; and instils in you a lively curiosity about those who differ from the herd. They are living differently, according to different norms, and so are making something of their lives, not simply falling into the borrowed lives of conformity. They are rounded individuals because they are able to conduct the kind of dialogue with their times that forges a distinctive voice.

Wilde's individuality, then, is a synthesis of his dependency and independence. He called himself an individualist, but that is different from the individualism of more recent times. The individualist does not ride roughshod

Figure 12 Oscar Wilde in 1882.

over others, like a patrician in his carriage who shows callous disregard for the plebs. Rather, the individualist is in the gutter of the age, too, only working with the materials to be found there, and creating a way of life that shines like a star for others.'

Another country

Wilde develops this philosophy in his essay on socialism. It's not a manifesto, or a piece of political philosophy in the usual sense. Rather, Wilde is painting a picture of a utopia. That, literally, means 'no place', for the aim of the exercise is to imagine an impossible but perfect society that, like an allegory, highlights flaws in the society that actually exists.

Wilde is against what has been called welfarism, the unintended consequence of the welfare state when people become so dependent upon the state that they are unable to make choices for themselves. They have no self-determination, and so are not able to act freely, as individuals. Charity undermines their individuality; collective largesse demoralizes them. Wilde uses colourful examples to make his point:

'Just as the worst slave-owners were those who were kind to their slaves, and so prevented the horror of the system being realized by those who suffered from it, and understood by those who contemplated it, so, in the present state of things in England, the people who do most harm are the people who try to do the most good.'

Wilde worries about an overbearing state, but he also worries about an overbearing market – the mechanism that has today run out of control. He imagines the effects of banning the possession of private property, for example. What this reveals is that private property too easily allows a small number of individuals to accrue wealth that is then not available to others. Their individualism is bought at the expense of others' individuality. The rich man is in his gaudy castle and the poor man is a no-man at the gate. (Substitute 'castle' for posh postcode and you have a fairly accurate picture of many cities in the modern world.) The poor aren't individuals but beasts of burden, tyrannized by the property owner's desires and wants:

'From [the poor's] collective force Humanity gains much in material prosperity. But it is only the material result that it gains, and the man who is poor is in himself absolutely of no importance. He is merely the infinitesimal atom of a force that, so far from regarding him, crushes him: indeed, prefers him crushed, as in that case he is far more obedient.'

Property undoes the rich too, Wilde continues, because it becomes their master. 'It involves endless claims upon one, endless attention to business, endless bother. If property had simple pleasures, we could stand it; but its duties make it unbearable.' The rich, therefore, are slaves too, only with better benefits. What they can't achieve is their individuality. By ignoring the peril of others, to whom they belong, they are demoralized too.

Individualism's conformity

In searching out the proper balance that leads to individuality, Wilde enjoys the paradoxes of the individualism that breeds a deep conformity. Celebrity culture is another feature of modern society that has grown, since his day, to monstrous proportions. These are the individuals, as elusive as Greek gods, upon whom many thousands, perhaps millions, of people project their desires and dreams. So few represent so much to so many. The worship they evoke is symptomatic of the conformity culture Wilde despised.

What happens is that individualism detaches people from the resources that can help to nurture true individuality. It's suspicious of faith and family, of class and community – and not without some reason, for in extreme, these things are oppressive. However, in the right balance, they offer deep soil for living. Consumerism's loam is thin. Acquisition replaces commitment; lifestyle does the same to traditions. Nothing much more than cash is required to participate. What's lost is the demand that deeper commitments make on you, coupled to the effort required to make them work for you. Without such engagement, the individual can make little of themselves.

'Through the Thou a person becomes I.'
Martin Buber

Individualism's fear

There's other odd characteristics about lopsided individualism. For example: it fears individuals with real individuality. This is arguably what did it for Wilde when he was sentenced to two years' imprisonment with hard labour in 1895. Following his release in 1897, and a move to Paris, he died, just three years later. You could say it was his character that killed him, the character that, because it drew on his times, spoke too powerfully to his times. It left his fellows feeling unbearably uncomfortable. Prophets are never welcome in their own town.

I suspect that the contemporary interest in vampires plays to a similar unease. Vampires are big right now, in TV programmes like *True Blood* and books like the *Twilight* novels. Interestingly, too, vampires are often depicted as sexually ambivalent aesthetes, like Wilde. The thing that freaks us about vampires is they are people who look exactly like us. We can even fall in love with them. Only they are different. They drink blood. And given half a chance, they'd suck the lifeblood out of us. They fascinate and threaten in equal measure by the combination of their individuality and dependence upon us.

Individualism, then, wants people to be the same, via their consumptive behaviour. It's odd, as nothing should be so abhorrent to it as the collective – though you don't have to be Sigmund Freud to know that the repressed returns in perverted guise. Market segmentation is not the same as individuality, and it's individuality that Wilde encourages us to nurture. Like writing, which demands observation, discernment and, perhaps most striking of all, self-discipline – striking because that's another characteristic of individuality which individualism denies. It's not freedom of choice per se that counts, but the freedom to make commitments – commitments to the realization of your own life, not at the expense of others.

A Step

The way of life that Wilde seeks could be likened to the difference between watching the television, listening to the radio, reading a book and writing a book. Watching TV is relaxing but it asks little of you as an individual. It's a collective experience, a kind of bubblegum for the brain, and leaves you calmed rather than nourished. Listening to the radio is a mass medium too, but it is more demanding. It requires an engagement of your imagination – some individuality – to make up for what sound alone can't convey.

Reading a book is a little more arduous again, as the words on the page need your attention. Further, it's between the lines that most of the work in great literature is done, and that work must be done by you. Great writers need good readers. And finally, writing a book – or essays or plays – is the most challenging task, the author taking on the tremendous burden of the creative process and the effort to speak to others. (Even for this apparently solitary task, others are, in fact, quite present.) If it goes right, though, the writer achieves their own voice, their own world, their own self: individuality.

So tonight, if your habit is the telly, try the radio. If it's the radio, try a book. And if it's a book, pick up that pen.

13

Love – or how to be seriously promiscuous

THE insights that can be gleaned about love from philosophy are deep and various; they can genuinely enhance our capacity to love and expand our perceptions of human desire. It's not that these insights will suddenly make love easy. If anything, they affirm that it's always easy to make mistakes in love; doing so is part of becoming a better lover.

Moreover, it's hard to think about love at the best of times. In fact, when it's going well, most don't think about it at all. It's when it goes badly, and particularly when it hurts, that love is revealed in all its labyrinthine complexity. However, a few ideas about love can help to tackle this particular Gordian knot. There is an art of loving, and it's an art that many philosophers have thought can be learned.

> 'Love interrupts at every hour the most serious occupations, and sometimes perplexes for a while even the greatest minds.'
> Arthur Schopenhauer

Lost halves

Plato was one such philosopher, arguably the first in the West to put love at the heart of his thought. He wrote a myth, ascribing it to a comic writer called Aristophanes, in which he proposed that originally human beings were shaped like large round spheres. They were then cut in half by the gods, the halves forming what we know as ourselves, men and women. Thus, we now wander the face of the Earth looking for our 'lost halves', and when we discover that person what a joy it is.

The myth gives expression to the mighty power of love. Its force was precisely what drew Plato to it. If anything in life needs handling well, love does. His mad story about bifurcated humans running around looking for another makes the point well. It's a picture of life all can recognize.

Plato   (428/427 BCE – 348/347 BCE)

Quick summary: In his youth, Plato might have been a wrestler, and he was supposed to become a politician. However, one day he met Socrates outside the theatre. He immediately dropped everything and followed the sage. Which is lucky for us, as he virtually invented Western philosophy in the process.

Key text: His ideas about love can be found in three of his dialogues in particular, the *Symposium*, *Phaedrus* and *Lysis*. The *Symposium* is an excellent place to start. It's both a great read and easily related to life.

Interesting fact: It's often assumed that ancient philosophy was just for men. However, Plato taught women in his school too, and called them 'philosopher-queens'.

The romantic myth

Plato's myth of lost halves tells us something else. Notice how it focuses on romantic love. That's striking because almost all the discussion of love in our culture has to do with romantic love, the business of finding a lover and falling in love. Such love is undoubtedly part of the story. But it's only a part – and not the part most people spend most of their lives enjoying, negotiating, or trying to survive. Rather, it's mature love that will occupy much of any life of love, or so most people would hope. And yet, the discussion of this love is often entirely missing.

Today you might blame that on the commercial mawkishness that perpetually plays on our desire for love, the industries that every year festoon the high street with pink hearts and Valentine's roses. They peddle the line that love is an experience that will transform your life. It can save you better than any god. But perhaps the problem is not so new.

For Plato, too, appears to have worried that the people of his day were treating love like a god and resisted worshipping it himself in that way. He argued that, if you deify love, it will rule you and ruin you. He did think that love was vitally important: one modern thinker has commented that Plato's philosophy might be better termed 'erosophy'. However, he believed that it is better to think of love not as a god but as that which can carry you towards the best things in life.

Figure 13
Greek love.

In the language of ancient mythology, Eros is neither immortal like a deity, nor mortal like us humans, but an intermediate between the two. Eros stands between gods and humans, conveying messages and gifts, particularly about the nature of what is beautiful, good and true.

What this suggests is that, at its best, love inspires us to strive for the higher things that we can devote our lives to. Plato argued that love is like a ladder which lifts you up. It enables an ever greater *joie de vivre*, an ever deeper engagement with life, until the good in life itself shines through. This is a kind of transcendence – a stepping beyond yourself because love is that which transcends our many limitations.

Higher love in practice

One of the most common ways in which this higher love is made manifest, Plato suggests, is in the bearing of children. Love is the beautiful thing that the parents share and when they come together, with seriousness and deliberation, they give birth to something that can be called very good – a child. In this procreativity the love of the parents becomes almost divine, and their love, as it is carried down through the generations, almost immortal.

There's reason for caution here: it is almost as easy to be overly romantic about children as about young love. Children do not always turn out to be as beautiful, good and true as the parents first hoped; they rebel and change. For many lovers, they turn out not to be a possibility at all. So if not children, then Plato suggests a kind of 'pregnancy of the soul or imagination' that issues in other kinds of creativity, perhaps works of art, poetry or even philosophy. A wise insight, he proposes, is like a 'child of the soul' that can never be lost.

This is a more expansive notion of love than purely romantic love, and it is enormously valuable for that reason. It points us beyond our immediate concerns, and nurtures the kind of love that looks to other people and things.

> *'Love does not consist in gazing at each other,*
> *but in looking outward together in the same*
> *direction.'*
>
> Antoine de Saint-Exupéry

How to be seriously promiscuous

What Plato is saying is that human beings are designed for love. To be human is to search for things that are lovely. In a certain way, he believes that it's good to be promiscuous – not to sleep around, but to cultivate the love that is in us. Be seriously promiscuous, he advises, not in taking more lovers, but in nurturing greater loves.

It might be called 'educating the heart'. It's about learning that love is far more than romantic feeling, far more than a rush of hormones to the head. Love is about embracing life.

Interestingly, it is also the case that love is ultimately not *found*; it is *made*. So much of the effort that people put into love these days seems to be in trying to make themselves lovable, whereas the question is really how capable of love you yourself are. That sounds blunt, but it is actually empowering. It implies that there is much you can do in pursuit of this life of love. Love is something that can be practised, much as you can practise being generous or kind. It's an activity, an attitude you can have as you step out into the world. It is not mostly a question of waiting for it to happen to you, as we're often told.

That takes time, courage and is often achieved in little things. The loving person, and the individual who is wise about love, is someone who has a developed character for love, a loving habit of the heart.

When lovey-doveyness gets annoying

When you think about it, Plato's ideas make clear sense. Psychologists have noticed that when two people meet, they are, by definition, strangers. If they then suddenly feel close to one another, and the walls between them come down – which is to say they start to fall in love – that is exhilarating. It seems wonderful and miraculous, not least for someone who has for some time being looking for the 'right person', their lost half. Sexual attraction is the powerful, physical expression of that new-found intimacy. Loneliness appears banished to memory.

However, falling in love cannot be lasting, by definition. This was the insight of one psychologist, Erich Fromm. It is premised on the meeting of strangers, he explains, so once you stop being a stranger to this new person, and they stop feeling delightfully strange to you, the feeling of falling for them, and its exhilaration, will ease off too. What was miraculous starts to feel humdrum. Next, it's easy to feel that, if you were falling *in* love, you've now fallen *out of* love; the temptation is to call the whole thing off. The danger is that people become addicted to falling in love and its thrills. Perhaps our culture has become addicted to it in this way too.

But Fromm said there is a different kind of love, which he called 'standing in love'. Unlike falling in love, which is premised on the fact that the lovers are still more or less strangers, to stand in love is to love a person because they are as well known to you as you are to yourself. It's joy is the delight of knowing another person and being known by them.

Just how unlike standing in love and falling in love are can be gleaned by thinking about the difference between being with individuals who are falling in love and with individuals who are standing in love. The first couple – the new lovers – are typically not much fun to be with. They are so in love with each other that they have little concern for anyone else. It's the lovey-dovey syndrome. It is deeply annoying to have to share an evening with them or sit opposite them on the train. They are so absorbed in each other that they do not notice the rest of the world. They think of love as a kind of luck and that their luck is in – and, conversely, that everyone else's luck is out. As a result, you feel alone when with them.

Being with people who are standing in love is entirely different. It is a joy. The nicest people to know are those who are in love with each other and who make you feel part of their love. Standing in love bids you welcome too. Such lovers have learned the art of love with each other and this results in care and concern for others.

We've said that love is complex. It can draw people together, and drive them apart. Consider that complexity by asking which of these thoughts you consider true, which false, which a bit of both.

Love begets love. **Love** doesn't run out. **Love** is blind. **Love** is mad. **Love** is short. **Love** means never having to say sorry. **Love** conquers all things. **Love** is the opposite of fear. **Love** is becoming one while remaining two. **Love** is not found; it is made. You do not fall in **love**, you stand in **love**. **Love** is giving more than receiving. **Love** is the combination of cunning and desire in the search for what you lack. **Love** is creativity inspired by the presence of beauty. **Love** is selfish genes longing to spread. **Love** is the irrational striving to live. **Love** is compassion. **Love** is the attempt to form friendship inspired by beauty. **Love** is the search for your lost half. **Love** kills the thing it loves. **Love** is not gazing at each other but gazing in the same direction. **Love** is a strategy for manipulation. **Love** is pathological. To **love** is to rejoice. Depression is the loss of the capacity to **love**. To **love** is to take pleasure. To **love** is to be happy that someone else exists. **Love** is care. **Love** is the rubbing of flesh and the excretion of slime. **Love** is good timing. **Love** hurts.

14

Me – being true to yourself

POLONIUS *makes it seem so simple. In Hamlet, Shakespeare has him say the now-famous words to his son, Laertes: 'This above all: to thine own self be true.' The formula rings like a Delphic injunction across an individualistic world, quite as powerfully as a sacred scripture. If only it were so simple.*

But it's not. What Polonius failed to tell his son is that your own self is hard to know, and, perhaps worse, is easy to mistake for an air brushed, imagined image. The switch is from being true to yourself, to being true to a fancied version of yourself. That is the nub of the challenge posed to us by the virtue of integrity. How might we achieve not what we'd like to be but what we are?

> 'To enter into your own mind you need to be armed to the teeth.'
> Paul Valéry

Carl Gustav Jung (1875–1961)

Quick guide: A Swiss psychiatrist, sometime colleague of Sigmund Freud, and founder of analytic psychology. He introduced the world to concepts such as extroversion, introversion, the collective unconscious and archetypes.

Key texts: *Memories, Dreams, Reflections* (1963) – a memoir – also
serves as a introduction to his thought.
Interesting fact: Jung argued that modern, technological people
see UFOs for much the same reasons as medieval people saw
angels. It's us imagining what cosmic benevolence, or malignancy,
might be like.

Circular individuation

Jung is just one thinker to offer a more subtle, and truer,
account of how an individual might achieve integrity. He called
it *individuation*. It's a circular process and proceeds by way of
integrating the different parts of the psyche. It's about self-
actualization, and as such is very different from the linear
process of self-realization that Polonius imagines.

Jung believed that human character falls across a spectrum
of opposite poles. There is the extrovert and introvert polarity,
as well as many others – the masculine and feminine principles,
those of reason and feeling, observation and intuition, and so
on. Typically, one pole is dominant in a personality, and the
other dominated, perhaps lost to the unconsciousness. This lost
pole makes itself felt in dreams, at times of stress, or during
experiences that are revelatory. The task of individuation is
permanently to recover those hidden elements and knit them
together into a whole. The watchword is *discovery*.

What is also discovered is that human beings are
simultaneously dependent and independent creatures. We are
dependent upon the influences of the past, for we are not the
authors of our own existence. Jung put it this way:

'Just as the body has an anatomical prehistory of millions
of years, so also does the psychic system. And just as the
human body today represents in each of its parts the result of
this evolution, and everywhere still shows traces of its earlier
stages – so the same may be said of the psyche.'

So we exercise our independence by shaping the past in
the present, and so steering a path into the future.

Our integrity, therefore, takes upon a particular character. Individuation is about taking responsibility for oneself. The person of integrity no longer blames parents or evolution or custom or necessity or the stars or God. Neither do they constantly look for distractions, routinely apologize for themselves, perpetually look over the garden fence, or enthuse about the latest next best thing. Rather, with individuation, your life has become your own, for good or ill. You take possession of it, and in so doing become self-determining. It's perhaps like the potter who takes clay and moulds an elegant jar. A good potter, using the same materials as all other potters across the ages, can create a style that is distinctly their own. The art of such potters, from Euxitheos to Grayson Perry, we say, has integrity. It is their unique synthesis of what the artist inherited. I has become me.

Pottery is hard. Individuation is harder. It is not a matter simply of stamping your mark on the world and having an assertive ego. Often, in fact, a Donald Trump will demonstrate all the neuroses of the narcissist, which is a problem not because they love themselves but because they *cannot* love themselves, and so constantly struggle to do so, acting that out on the public stage. It's a route that steps away from individuation. Instead, Jung explains, 'Individuation does not shut one out from the world, but gathers the world to oneself,' adding: 'I cannot blame the person who takes to his heels at once.' It's more about following a path to the centre of things, than a route to a high place upon which imperiously to survey the world. It's a kind of circumambulation of the self, as is reverently enacted in many religions when individuals walk around symbolic objects or places of veneration. Muslims walk around the Kaaba; Hindus circumnavigate a stuppa; Christians walk the circular labyrinths of medieval cathedrals, symbolising the 'soul-struggle' involved in the journey of life.

The role of the daimon

A great challenge is how to envisage this process, not least in an age that has become detached from the old symbols of individuation. One way that Jung developed concerned what he called his *daimon*. When reflecting upon the troubles life had brought him, not least falling out with his one-time mentor and friend, Sigmund Freud, Jung wrote this:

'I have had much trouble getting along with my ideas. There was a daimon in me, and in the end its presence proved decisive. It overpowered me, and if I was at times ruthless it was because I was in the grip of the daimon. I could never stop at anything once attained. I had to hasten on, to catch up with my vision. Since my contemporaries, understandably, could not perceive my vision, they saw only a fool rushing ahead.'

The daimon that Jung detected felt like an entity with which he had to struggle to become himself. It might also be called the unconscious or the divine, he reflected, because it is that which is not contained or controlled by us consciously, but instead springs from another part of life – the part with which we must achieve a synthesis. For that reason, it appears strange to us, as if acting of its own accord, perhaps as if numinous. To put it another way, our daimons are largely unknown to us, the process of their discovery being precisely what individuation aims to achieve.

The value of personifying these elements that are so mysterious to us is that we can gain a sense of the life they contain and how we might engage with them. It's as if we step out of ourselves to engage with ourselves. That will typically feel troubling, dramatic and fragmenting. As another ancient story of individuation involving a daimon has it – that of Jacob wrestling with the angel in the Hebrew Bible – Jacob was left after the experience with a dislocated hip. He is damaged. But what's happening is this: 'The whole man is challenged and enters the fray with his whole reality. Only then can he become whole.'

Moral heroes

The ancient Greek philosophers envisaged integrity by way of daimons too. The thought is implicit in the word that is often translated as 'happiness': *eudaimonia*. It literally has to do with the 'good daimon' – embodying the good daimon that belongs to you. It was sometimes envisaged in the iconography of the Greek demigod Silenus. Potters would make busts of this companion of Dionysus, concealing inside the clay a small figurine of gold. That could be revealed only if the pottery was broken, representing the need to shatter the external, rough-hewn individual in the struggle for integrity. In the Bible, a not dissimilar course is imagined in the saying that unless someone loses their life, they will not gain it.

The translation of *eudaimonia* as 'happiness' is, therefore, almost entirely unhelpful. The Greeks knew that pleasure was part of the good life. Being true to yourself, though, is not much concerned with heightened emotional states, as happiness implies today. Rather, *eudaimonia* was being in a state of integrity. It is a condition and a feeling, in the sense of 'being right' – an often tough moral determination.

The great exemplars of integrity were the heroes of ancient Greek drama. They were individuals who had discovered what they ought to do and moreover did it – even as the chorus on stage, and the other characters, implored them not to. These moral heroes and heroines sacrifice themselves for their integrity (the 'losing oneself' motif again), as Iphigenia does when she dies to appease Artemis. Their lives are tragic, and for that reason venerated. The audience can only hope that innate within them they would find the integrity to do the same, should it be demanded of them.

Animal daemons

The novelist Philip Pullman offers a brilliant modern myth of daimons in the *His Dark Materials* trilogy. The children in the story all have what he refers to as 'daemons'. They are represented in the form of animals that follow their child closely, mutating and changing. This happens because their character has not yet settled, just as the child's vocation in life has not either. When they achieve adulthood, though, the daemons become fixed, a process called 'settling'. Having reached the moment when they must decide whom they want to be, they then embark on a new stage in life's journey which seeks to actualize it – to become who they are.

Similarly, in the story, there is no worse fate than to be separated from your daemon because, for humans, this is to be separated from your chance to live a self-determined life – the chance to have integrity, to become yourself. Children in the story who suffer this fate lose their substance, become monstrous, or simply die.

Figure 14
Lady with an Ermine
(c.1489–90) by
Leonardo da Vinci.

Vocation calls

We mentioned vocation, and this is another way of conceptualizing the process. The person who follows their vocation is someone who engages with life wholeheartedly. When with them, you sense they are present, not absent, and they leave you feeling more present too – or longing to be so. Their lives have a sense of weight, expansiveness and movement. So following a vocation, and often having to work hard to discern the direction it will take you, is also to be 'thrust on to the road of individuation'. It often generates profound inner confrontations, as opposites within you collide. But that process too promotes personal growth – integrity – and so comes to be experienced as a great source of energy, creativity and insight. A blessing.

Unsurprisingly, the life of the artist provides many excellent analogies too. The painter Wassily Kandinsky described it in his book *Concerning the Spiritual in Art*. His vocation was to 'harmonize the whole', and it was in the arena of personal discipline, as much as on the canvas, that this harmonization had to be achieved. This explains why Kandinsky talks about the artist's life using the language of suffering and fear as much as anything else:

'The artist is not born to a life of pleasure. He must not live idle; he has a hard work to perform, and one which often proves a cross to be borne. He must realize that his every deed, feeling, and thought are raw but sure material from which his work is to arise, and he is free in art but not in life.'

'A creative person has little power over his own life,' concurred Jung. 'He is not free. He is captive and driven by his daimon.' Though, of course, while things don't work out as you planned them, the unexpected delivers much more besides. You may not believe it at times, but your vocation is in your own best interests.

> 'The chief requirement of the good life, is to live without any image of oneself.'
> Iris Murdoch

The shadow

One final concept from Jungian psychology offers another reflection on individuation, and suggests something to try out. This is the shadow – that cluster of elements from which you are separated and to which individuation would have you joined. Jung put it like this:

'The shadow personifies everything that the subject refuses to acknowledge about himself and yet is always thrusting itself upon him directly or indirectly – for instance, inferior traits of character and other incompatible tendencies.'

It is another manifestation of your daimon, the dark side of yourself that it takes effort to engage, understand, unpick.

Because it tends to be refused and repressed, it will constantly return, exercising an influence on your life that you might hardly recognize. It can, though, be a source of profound self-understanding. The shadow is the place that you experience revelations. Revealing those insights is the main task of Jungian therapy. And there are other ways in which the shadow can show itself to you too.

A Step

The thing to try, then, is to engage your shadow by going to places where you feel uncomfortable, or that challenge you. It may be that you have a shadow friend, an individual with whom you have a love/hate relationship. They annoy you, and yet tell you something important about yourself too. Another kind of shadow experience can be over that about which you routinely get panicked or angry, perhaps when asked to do certain things, or when you're kept waiting, or at certain moments of the week. Why are you annoyed? What's the trigger? What's that shadow moment telling you about your daimon? Or again, you may decide to go somewhere, or do something, that has always drawn you, though it makes you wary too. It might be calling a half-forgotten or estranged relative, reading the work of someone you regard as a sworn enemy, or even fixing up some therapy.

It'll be a struggle. It'll be painful to have your vanity cast into its shadow. But it might be the key to more life, to integrity. Or at least a clue.

15

Meaning – or why it's good to talk

WE'RE *between the beasts and the angels. This was a thought had by Saint Augustine, the great theologian. He meant that we humans are 'in between' creatures. We are animals, but we're unlike other animals too. It's tricky to say precisely how, not least because our understanding of other animals is always growing, and there might not be absolute differences. But that there are differences is obvious. Which other animal picks up a book on how to live?*

But we're not angels. We're referring here to those mythological entities, the beings that exist outside space and time and, in Augustine's scheme at least, stand before God, which is to say that they stand before the good, the beautiful and the true. We may, on occasions, receive intimations of such delights. But we mostly see through a glass darkly. Our vision is just one part of us that is not 'angelic'.

The question, then, is how to understand our animal/angel status? If we're in between, what does that mean for how we should live? The questions are confusing, and the answers are not entirely clear. But they're important to raise nonetheless.

> '. . .of all the differences between man and the lower animals, the moral sense or conscience is by far the most important. . . it is summed up in that short but imperious word ought, so full of high significance.'
>
> Charles Darwin

Herbert McCabe   (1926–2001)

Quick summary: A Dominican monk, McCabe lived at Blackfriars in Oxford and was the kind of don who profoundly affected everyone he encountered. He was an expert both on Thomas Aquinas and Ludwig Wittgenstein.

Key text: An excellent introduction to the good life is his book that goes by that name. It's written in McCabe's characteristically lucid, witty and penetrating style.

Interesting fact: He used to get into trouble with the Church authorities, once being banned from editing a journal. When, a few years later, he took up the editorship again, he began his first piece by writing: 'As I was saying before I was so oddly interrupted. . .'

. . . .

The talking animal

There is a story Herbert McCabe tells, in an essay on animals, about a Victorian clergyman whose memoirs record him one day looking out of the vicarage window. He spotted a wonderful bird, displaying brilliant plumage, moving with great grace, and looking like nothing he had seen before. The clergyman then wrote this: 'However, while I went to get my gun it flew away.'

Today, it seems natural to treat the beasts of the earth and air with respect, even if in practice we are inconsistent in doing so. That respectful attitude has deepened as our knowledge of their behaviour and lives has deepened – though it might be noted that much of our knowledge stems from work done by

Victorians who also observed animals down the barrel of a gun. It seems very likely, now, that some animals can love, grieve and take pleasure in ways strikingly similar to our own loving, grieving and pleasure-taking. We understand the powerful notion of cruelty to animals, and how pervasive an evil it is.

There is a difference between us and them, though, and it's called *language*. Animals belong to a biological species. Humans belong to a biological species and a linguistic community – which is to say that we are constituted by our political and social association, as well as by our biology, and we are able to respond to and modify them both. 'When the human animal appears on the scene,' McCabe wrote, 'the extraordinary (and so far inexplicable) thing that happens is the emergence of language.'

Figure 15 Human beings have often ascribed meaning to beasts, as in this sixteenth-century Bestiary. Animals, fortunately, do not return the compliment.

Meaning matters

It might immediately be objected that the most recent research raises the possibility that other animals have language too. Birds sing, dogs bark and monkeys can manipulate symbols. But here's the difference: language is not primarily a set of noises; it is a set of signs. And while monkeys can apparently utilize a few of these signs, when portrayed as pictures and colours, they can do so only because the human animal invented them first.

This leads to something else, to do with meaning. For to have meaning is to enter into a language and, because language is social, thereby also a community. We are social animals like other social animals, as Aristotle pointed out, but also *unlike* them. We don't just behave instinctively but, sometimes at least, consciously and reflectively too. Further, while my thoughts are my thoughts, meaning is found in the way in which language transcends my individuality; it connects me with something bigger than myself: the linguistic community. When we learn a language, we don't just learn words and grammar, but we discover that we can participate in a tradition. In a strange way, we don't just speak words; they speak *us* too.

McCabe unpacks these thoughts further by exploring how our 'sensitive life', which is the experience that comes from having senses, differs from other animals. The main difference is not of kind but of *intensity*, and intensity meant in a certain way. It's not primarily along an axis of pleasure and pain, though human animals may well be able to experience pains and pleasures that other animals do not as a result of language – existential agonies, aesthetic delights, and the like. But rather, we can transcend our experience, to some degree, in language. Think of that characteristically human artefact we call literature.

Language adds a new dimension to the experience of life. McCabe calls this dimension *understanding*: linguistic animals, such as ourselves, understand in a way that non-linguistic animals don't. Like my dog, I enjoy my food. Unlike my dog, I understand why I wait until set times in the day to be fed. Not that our understanding is complete. We may be higher than the beasts, but we're lower than the angels. Humility is the appropriate response, not hubris.

What then is it to have such a life, beyond the mere experiencing of sensations? It is the ability to find abstract meaning in the world. Animals interpret the world via their senses and to that extent do live in meaningful worlds. Plants, presumably, do not. This might be called *sensual meaning*. However, language adds something new as it is based not on the senses alone but on an intellectual and linguistic interpretation of the world as well. That requires a certain biological substratum – like vocal cords and a brain – but it primarily exists in the non-biological worlds of stories, myths, history and tradition.

> *'All animals, except man, know that the principal business of life is to enjoy it.'*
> Samuel Butler

The nine senses

Today there is a huge debate about to what degree humans are in control of their linguistic world of meaning – whether or not we follow reason, say, or exercise free will. There is a fashionable tendency to play these capacities down to almost nothing, to say that we are not free and that reason is a delusion. It's better, McCabe suggests, to step back from the muddle. He borrows from Thomas Aquinas to do so.

In addition to the five biological senses, this other Dominican of the twelfth century proposed that we need to add four more. These extra senses are a bit like the senses we infer when we say 'That makes no sense' or ask 'Is that sensible?' They are:

1 **The 'co-ordinating sense'** This generates meaning out of the five separate biological senses. For example, our eyes don't snap images like a camera, but rather co-ordinate with our whole selves, and thus we see.
2 **The sense of recollection** This can also be called the 'imagination'. It remembers previous sensations and folds them in too.
3 **The 'evaluative sense'** This assesses and weighs up significance.
4 **The 'memory'** This positions us in a temporal world.

What difference do these four additional senses make to us? Well, have you ever asked yourself why is it so hard to throw a baby on a fire, and yet apparently so easy to fly a plane over a village in Vietnam and release napalm on the babies beneath, smothering them in flames. It's because the first action engages our five animal senses, and so violently repels us, whereas the second does not, being performed from the vantage of a few hundred feet. In order to be repelled by the bombing, we must use our imaginations, we must engage our trust in meaning. As McCabe sums up: 'Behaviour that is the fruit of language [like bombing] needs to be controlled by language, by reason.' It's why we need ethics, and other animals apparently don't. They need only their senses.

The distinguishing feature of language is that it enables us to step back from our experience, at least to a degree. But only to step back, not escape. Moreover, we need our senses to help us make decisions too, as meaning arises in dialogue with them. Humans are the animals that have invented language, but we are still animals. That heritage persists.

Being embodied

Let's look at our nature in another way, and consider our animal status and its meaning by contrast with machines. It's tempting to think of living creatures as machines because, since the seventeenth century, science has proceeded largely on that basis and achieved a huge variety of fascinating and useful results. However, it is easy to lose sight of the fact that science adopted that model of what it is to be a living creature only out of convenience. The model of the machine has proven to be an immensely valuable pragmatic assumption, but it should not be confused with what we are in truth. For we are not machines. Why not?

McCabe defines a machine as an imitation animal. A machine, for example, has the capacity to move itself, as we do. However, we are much more than automobiles – automobile meaning 'self-moving'. Think of the car, now that we've mentioned them. They are built from a number of elements: wheels, gears, chassis, pistons. Each element can be accounted for by the way it relates to the other elements. There was a song, I recall, called 'Dry Bones' that made seductively similar observations about the human 'machine', when it observed how the backbone is connected to the thighbone, and the thighbone is connected to the knee bone, and so on. However, the car needs something else to make sense of it, which no amount of analysis of its parts and their links will reveal. That's because it's an element that is not part of the machinery at all. It's the driver. The driver is the non-mechanical part of the car that fundamentally explains the mechanism.

To put it more generally, machines need non-machines to make sense of them. It is we who give them meaning. It's why, if you see a watch lying on the ground, it's quite natural to ask whom it belongs to and who made it. Animals, though, are different. Unlike cars, we are autonomous movers. We are not driven by any external driver, but by our own desires and impulses, which are part of us. Similarly, our 'parts' are not really machine-like parts at all. For example, while it makes perfect sense to say that a wheel rolls, it does not make any sense to say that a leg walks. Rather, we, the whole creature, are what walks. We need legs to walk, of course. But we need far more than legs to do so – roughly, in fact, the whole of us: eyes to see, ears to balance, arms to swing, lungs to breathe, brains to decide, lives to live with meaning.

Body work

Why does this matter? For one thing, it means that we should treat our bodies with reverence, as they are not composed of discardable parts. One perhaps does not need to worry too much about placing one's nail clippings in the bin. But it is striking how much psychological, as well as physiological, care is taken of individuals who undergo transplant surgery. It's a major trauma not solely because of the surgery, but also because of the gift of themselves that one person makes to another. It's why the surgery feels so meaningful.

How we treat our bodies also plays a major part in how we try to live well. It is not the case that we can ignore our bodies in our pursuit of the good life, and concentrate mostly on the soul or mind. 'My soul is not me,' noted Thomas Aquinas. 'I am this living material body,' continues McCabe.

A great example of how the good life involves taking care of the body in harmony with the mind or soul is found in sport. The sportsperson doesn't just need to be in great physical shape, but emotional and mental shape too. It's also striking that sportspeople deploy a particular kind of language when describing their way of life. They talk about excellence, training, skill and capabilities. This is the same language that the virtue ethics approach to the good life utilizes – virtues being a synonym for excellences. It's a holistic approach to the good life, unlike, say, the approaches to ethics that treat the good life as a series of questions about what is right and wrong, to be settled as a rational process in the mind.

A Step

Our embodiment makes us like other animals, though we are more than machines. Language makes us unlike other animals, and a little closer to the angels. Meaning and understanding is the result. So the step is to celebrate our in-between status, to sense it.

Think of some recent new words — defriending, neuromythology, agroterrorism, blowback, twonk — and use one today in a sentence. You're participating in that extraordinary creative capacity of our species. You're celebrating the richness of a tradition, of which Shakespeare is the patron saint, and to which you're an heir. You're giving, and finding, meaning in the world.

16

Money – our frozen desire

THE *first thing to say about money is that it's a great good. That's a necessary starting point as it's so easy, particularly in books about morality, to indulge in abhorrence of the filthy lucre. That's a cathartic activity but misguided. Money is too subtle to be treated so simply. Money is the root of a lot of good, and it's worth saying that before dwelling on how it might also be the root of a lot of evil. If money is the new religion, it's like the old religions too – good in parts.*

As any student of history will confirm, progress in human civilization has always gone hand in hand with progress in financial markets. Inasmuch as it is a cause of many ills, that's partly because we forget how it contributes to the common good. Keeping a keen eye on what money is for is crucial. So, we've a simple question: what is money?

> 'Money, it turned out, was exactly like sex, you thought of nothing else if you didn't have it and thought of other things if you did.'
> James Baldwin

John Maynard Keynes (1883–1946)

Quick summary: Keynes is the originator of Keynesianism, the theory that governments should spend during periods of recession, and increase taxes during periods of prosperity, to iron out the booms and busts of the economic cycle.

Key text: A humane introduction to his thought is found in his short essay, 'Economic Possibilities for Our Grandchildren' – for we are his grandchildren now.

Interesting fact: Though Keynes was an economist, it was because he didn't regard himself as an economist, but as a philosopher and historian, that paradoxically made him so great: he strove to understand humanity first, markets second.

Good relationships

If there's one word that might sum up Keynes's conception of what money is, it would be the word *relationship*. Money is a subtle means human beings devise to mediate their relationships between one another, and also between themselves and the future. That makes immediate sense when you think about the language we use to talk about money. People worry about the 'collapse of trust' or the 'need for confidence'. Almost exactly the same language is used to describe what's happening during an economic downturn as is used to discuss a failed marriage.

When it comes to the first relationship, how we relate to one another, money is one way that we exchange things of value between ourselves. It makes life easier in the process because it means we don't all have to bake bread, construct shelters and stitch shoes. Instead, we just have to do one of those things, and buy the rest from others. Plus, because we can learn to do one thing well, we can become very efficient at doing it, and so buy ourselves free time too.

When it comes to the future, money is one way that we try to protect ourselves against adverse things that might happen; money is a store of protection against fate, which we accumulate ahead of time. This is done in fancier ways than simply storing gold under the mattress. Alongside the emergence of civilization, history shows the emergence of financiers, who are a particularly inventive breed of humans. They devise securities, insurance and bonds. As if by a process of alchemy, that in itself leads to the increase of money, and so capital grows – which in turn powers civilization.

The story of money should be a happy one. But it's not. So what goes wrong?

Bad relationships

The key, again, is found in the word *relationship*. For our relationships with one another are often ambivalent, and our relationship with the future is radically uncertain.

When money gets caught up in human relationships, which it does by definition, then it becomes more than just a neutral medium of exchange. It affects our beliefs, values and feelings about relationships too. Just watch a kid's face light up upon receipt of pocket money, or how adult heads turn as a Ferrari purrs down the high street. Money of itself can provoke all the extremes of human interaction, from jealousy to delight.

John Ruskin caught the dynamic well when he wrote: 'The force of the

Figure 16
The Fortune Teller
(1633–9) by the
French painter
Georges de La
Tour – an allegorical
warning about
money.

guinea you have in your pocket depends wholly on the default of a guinea in your neighbour's pocket. If he did not want it, it would be of no use to you.' Schopenhauer put it even more succinctly when he called money 'frozen desire'.

This leads to another dynamic. In the same way that we seek more from our relationships with other human beings, we being social animals, so we desire more money. The difference is that whereas relationships are an end in themselves, money should be treated as a means to an end. Only it's very easy to become confused about that. Money in the bank should not make us happy, as it does precisely nothing for us. And yet it does. More money makes us more happy.

The reason for this is that human desires are insatiable. We are the creatures that want more. It's both a curse and a blessing – a curse when not having more frustrates us; a blessing when seeking more stokes our creativity, resourcefulness and love of life.

Keynes realized that there are two kinds of needs that human beings have. Some are *absolute* needs, like bread, shelter and shoes. Others, however, are *relative* needs, like pocket money and Ferraris, and our desire for them tends to increase as people around us have an increase of them too. Moreover, even absolute needs take on the characteristic of relative needs. We don't just want bread but focaccia; not just shelter but a residence; not just shoes but Manolo Blahniks. (So don't believe those psychologists who say that individual happiness doesn't increase when incomes rise above £17,000, though individual unhappiness may well do.)

Moreover, just as our desire for better relationships can lead us to ruin the relationships we have already, because we become too demanding, so our desire for more money can lose us the little we have. This was the fate behind Plato's myth of the lost city of Atlantis. The fabled island-state overreached itself and sank into the sea 'in a single day and night of misfortune'.

Unknown unknowns

That tale of the unexpected leads us to why money can mess things up when it comes to that other relationship it mediates, between ourselves and the future. Behind Keynes's conception of money here is another important insight, namely that the future is radically uncertain.

He wrote a lot about probability and argued that most of the possibilities that lie ahead of us can't be measured with any degree of accuracy. It's like the weather. Mostly, we just don't know. Probabilities, therefore, are often just expressions of a feeling or hunch; it's quite likely to happen, or it's quite likely not to happen.

It is striking just how uncertain Keynes thought the future was, particularly when you remember that many of the things we do with our money – buy mortgages, invest in pensions, speculate on markets – are based upon the assumption that the future is pretty certain, not least that wealth will increase. It's more sensible, Keynes thought, to think of money as a way of guarding yourself against future shocks, not as a means of guaranteeing certain futures for yourself, be that a leisurely retirement on the golf course or the freedom at last to write your novel. You may well improve your handicap in your dotage. You may even put pen to paper. But equally, golf courses may become scarce due to water shortages, and that novel may prove beyond your reach. Darkness is ever before us. Money isn't light, just some protection. And remember, only *some*. If the uncertainties of the future are unbounded, then the temptation is to take out one insurance policy after another, after another, after another. . .

> '*Wine maketh merry; but money answereth all things.*'
> Ecclesiastes

Cash addicts

The complicated thing about money, then, is that it causes evil for precisely the same reason that it brings great goods. It so easily becomes a substitute for relationships because it is itself a form of relationship. The trouble is that money likes having the monopoly. Hence, this tendency to draw all value towards itself, and suck the value out of other relationships in the process.

We seem to have reached a particularly dire moment in the management of these tensions today. There's a common assumption that hard-working people can't be expected to show restraint in the pursuit of their financial goals. We are all Don Juans when it comes to cash. People routinely say, 'I was made an offer I couldn't refuse.' Money trumps all values. And if it's true that we live in a world in which people can't refuse money, then we live in a world of money addicts. Like sex addicts, we need a particularly strong form of therapy to get us off it, though just what that therapy might be is, as yet, far from clear.

To put it another way, money becomes its own end. That sheds light on the situation following the economic collapse of 2008. The thing that drives big bankers is not the wealth or the power but the banking itself. Money is the thing to which they are married. The relationship is one of passion – and apparently less easily dissolved than actual matrimony. Hence, bankers don't regard their errors as mistakes, but as a move in a game of love. If the move didn't have the expected outcome no one's to blame; the correct response is to make another move. Similarly, the bankers whom the public has asked to feel sorry will never do so. It makes no more sense than apologizing for being in love. Would you deny a relationship that mattered to you?

The art of living

Keynes worried about this predicament in his essay 'Economic Possibilities for Our Grandchildren'. He believed that humankind was on the verge of solving a problem that it had faced since it was walking the savannah, namely the economic problem of how to provide for its needs. He thought that in the early decades of the twenty-first century – about now – most people in the UK, and other parts of the developed world, would be earning enough money to live the good life. Economic growth, which has been accelerating since Drake sailed in the *Golden Hind*, would reach a point when it could supply all our needs. And would this be good? Probably not. It would likely as not provoke a crisis.

Humankind's entire *raison d'être* would have to change. Across centuries, until now, our ancestors' days were drenched with the sweat of their toil. Now, though, we need sweat no more – or not much – and can instead sing. And yet, Keynes noted, 'How few of us can sing!'

Money, having liberated us, could again imprison us, before we even had the chance to be free. Keynes continued: 'It will be those peoples, who can keep alive, and cultivate into a fuller perfection, the art of life itself and do not sell themselves for the means of life, who will be able to enjoy the abundance when it comes.' If our relationship with money frees us, will we know how to nurture our relationship to life?

It looks like we don't. The problem is that money is possessive. It is a jealous lover. Like being in an abusive relationship, it feels more consoling to stay with what you know than to attempt to break free of the habitual cycles of work. Three hours a day, Keynes calculated, should be enough for us. Do we work less than our grandparents? Quite the opposite.

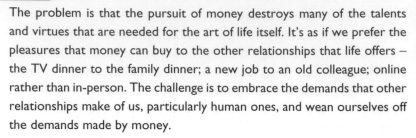

A Step

The problem is that the pursuit of money destroys many of the talents and virtues that are needed for the art of life itself. It's as if we prefer the pleasures that money can buy to the other relationships that life offers – the TV dinner to the family dinner; a new job to an old colleague; online rather than in-person. The challenge is to embrace the demands that other relationships make of us, particularly human ones, and wean ourselves off the demands made by money.

At the end of his essay, Keynes identifies some of the vices that we'd have to ditch to achieve the liberation that economic growth promises – we would have to recognize 'that avarice is a vice, that the exaction of usury is a misdemeanour, and the love of money is detestable'. As to the virtues, we'd have to learn to not worry so much about tomorrow, and hence not fear for the limitless uncertainties that money tells us it can insure us against. We'd have to learn to prefer the good over the useful; to love the enjoyment of what's before us right now. The question is: Can you do it?

17

Mourning — and avoiding depression

Loss sits close to life. The two hold hands like fated lovers. It has always been so. When Shakespeare writes, 'Grief fills the room up of my absent child, Lies in his bed, walks up and down with me,' we know the pain, we fear it. It's universal. And it's not just in the major losses of life that we experience the forfeit of life. Loss is with us from the moment of birth, birth being the first great loss, the loss of the warm intimacy of the womb. Crunch a brown leaf, expel a long breath, fall into a still sleep. Little losses accompany us like gathering shadows.

But I suspect that we're not as good at loss today as our ancestors were. The agony of death was more present before the birth of modern medicine. That familiarity would not have lessened the pain, but it would have stressed the crucial necessity of mourning. Death rites, from quietly lighting a candle to black displays of grief, would have been far more common than today. Now, death is different. There's truth in the truism that it's a taboo subject. Our rites of death are like thin watercolours compared to the thick oils of yesteryear's wailing. Who washes the body of their beloved any more? Few even welcome the corpse back into their home.

It matters, not only for the mourning we must undergo when we face our own great losses, which will come for all the blessings of science. But for the little losses too. Psychoanalysis understands the risk we face, because if you can't mourn, as we all must, you become melancholic. The difference is this. The mourner knows what they've lost. The melancholic does not. They cannot mourn, and instead fall into a pervasive depression, internalizing despair so that they despair of themselves.

Depression is pandemic in the modern world. It is not just that we diagnose it better, for the evidence is that it is actually spreading. Could the problem be that we are losing the art of mourning? Might the truth be that life would be richer if, instead of denying our losses, we embraced them?

> 'Now, with sullen shingle beaches wearing out
> the Tuscan sea, practise wisdom.'
>
> Horace

Melanie Klein (1882–1960)

Quick summary: A British psychoanalyst who developed what is known as object relations theory, the notion that life, particularly in childhood, is a process of learning that 'objects', notably parents, are separate from yourself, the subject.

Key text: A fascinating discussion of Klein, and the idea that mourning is of crucial importance, is found in Darian Leader's *The New Black: Mourning, Melancholia and Depression* (2008).

Interesting fact: Klein was a follower of Sigmund Freud, though she came into sharp conflict with Freud's daughter, Anna, over their different ideas about child psychology.

The art of mourning

The distinction between mourning and melancholy comes from Freud. He noticed that his melancholic patients suffered from profound experiences of loss, though unlike his patients who were successfully if painfully mourning, the melancholics couldn't understand what they were missing. It might be a loved one. It might be a loss of public standing. It might be a political or religious belief – a loss of faith. But for some reason, the specifics of the loss was too painful for them to stare in the face. They couldn't get a handle on what had happened. Though they might know the *facts* of their loss, the individual did not know the *significance* of what they had lost. Just that it was terrible. Consider the difference between the two.

The film *Truly, Madly, Deeply* (1990) is a wonderful portrayal of mourning. Nina has lost her lover, Jamie. The experience is almost overwhelming, and she is beginning to slip into the depression of melancholia – a risk that all mourners face – when suddenly Jamie returns. It's not quite clear whether it's his ghost or her imagination, but what the experience allows her to do is understand what she has lost.

She experiences all manner of unexpected feelings at his return. Delight, rage, hurt, consolation. Mourners know that too. But not depression. In particular, she realizes that while Jamie's loss will always pain her, and her life will have a little less music in it than before, she has not lost everything. In fact, as Jamie hangs around the house, Nina becomes quite infuriated with him. She leaps out of her skin at his sudden appearances. He brings his annoying dead friends around to watch videos. He turns up the central heating. When Nina meets Mark, and begins to fall for him, she can't quite tell Jamie to go, though she does let him go. She has mourned his loss.

The experience of melancholia

Melancholy, on the other hand, is captured in the almost unbearably moving film *I've Loved You So Long* (2008). It tells the story of Juliette, who has just been released from prison after a 15-year sentence. She goes to stay with her sister's family, and for most of the film the viewer is aware that something terrible has happened, though it is unclear what. Watching the film is, therefore, to experience something of melancholia's depression.

Figure 17 Dürer, Albrecht (1471–1528), *Melancholia I*. Engraving, 240×187mm, Stadelmusseum, Frankfurt am Main.

Juliette can't secure a job, though she's highly qualified. She can only manage a platonic relationship with a man she meets, who then suddenly disappears without explanation, deepening the sense of loss. Her affection for her niece is interrupted by the distress of her brother-in-law, who can't cope with Juliette being with her. Juliette and her sister visit their mother, who is lost too, to Alzheimer's disease. The tension rises as the viewer becomes desperate, desperate to know what's happened. Juliette, though, can't say what it is, not because she doesn't know why she was imprisoned, but because she can't get a handle on what her crime means. It is literally *unspeakable*.

The facts are appalling too. Eventually, it becomes clear that she has murdered her six-year-old son. She had reason to do so, as he had a terminal disease that would result in a lingering death. But for a mother to kill her child is a sin against nature, beyond comprehension. Her depression begins to lift only when, finally, she is able to tell her sister what happened. Her melancholia becomes mourning. Her feelings find a means of articulation. At last, she weeps.

> '*Blessed are those who mourn. For they shall be comforted.*'
> Matthew 5:4

The depressive position

Klein deepened Freud's ideas about mourning to show that it is part of everyday life, not just its calamitous moments. The reason for this is that loss starts young, in the dynamics between the child and its mother. Symbolically, it is expressed in terms of the relationship the child has to the breast. The breast can be both good and bad. The good breast is the one that offers warm sustenance and affection. The bad breast is the one that is not there when hunger and loneliness strike. The child, therefore, can metaphorically be said both to love and hate the breast. It is present and it is lost.

A crucial moment of development comes when the child realizes that the good and bad breast are one and the same. This precipitates a whole range of complex feelings. There is aggression, because the child will feel guilty at loathing what it also loves. That leads to a sense of sadness, and then concern, as the child tries to make up for its aggressive attitude towards what it longs for more than anything. Klein called this the *depressive position*. It's the moment when the pattern for future experiences of loss are set down, be they the future major losses of loved ones, or the future little losses of what the individual desires and once had – public standing, faith, youth, friends. The art of mourning, then, is the ability to negotiate the depressive position. Using the symbolic language again, the child must recognize that the breast, and its mother, are objects to which it is both attached and independent from. That is the balance to get right. It is painful, as it admits of no easy resolution. If the child hasn't learned it when young, it may find mourning difficult when older, and so slip into melancholia and depression. Every experience of loss will return the individual to the first loss, and since loss is part of life, being good at mourning is essential.

Rites of mourning

Klein also recognize that loss is a collective experience. This is sensed when a loss can overcome not just an individual but a whole society. It explains what happened in Britain when Princess Diana died. The fields of wilting flowers that appeared within hours outside the royal palaces, and the way time seemed to slow for a week, were described at the time as hysterical. But perhaps a less hysterical interpretation is to suggest that we were all, for a while, revisiting our own experiences of loss.

Entire streets of people emptied to line the route from the place of Diana's funeral to the site of her burial, drawn to pay homage to her body like pilgrims, and the action spoke of a deep desire to mourn. It was arguably an entirely healthy event, a rare occasion in the modern world at which people could mourn and did not evade their loss.

Klein realized that personal mourning is greatly helped when the individual realizes that others are mourning too. 'Nature mourns with the mourner,' she noted. That's the danger in a world that tries to bury mourning as well as the dead. We are left isolated, like the child in the depressive position who cannot understand what's going on. Rites of mourning are so important because their actions embody the art of mourning prepared for us by those who have gone before us. Going to the funeral, doing the 'traditional thing', allowing time to feel angry, hurt, elated, sad, is good.

Giving things up

The implications of being able to mourn run much further than being able to cope with grief, and so avoid depression. Klein's depressive position, the moment when you realize some things are different from you and beyond your control, is a moment that we face throughout adult life. The individual who finds it hard to give things up, from fatty hamburgers to the use of a car – feeling that without them life would be too depressing

– is perhaps not very good at mourning, at loss. It's striking that along with depression, obesity and traffic congestion are modern as pandemics too. Klein's thought suggests there's a link: mourning.

The capacity for empathy, stepping into another's shoes, is linked to the depressive position as well. It's only when we can recognize that someone is separate from us, and cope with the mix of feelings that separateness precipitates – feelings of fear and aggression as well as love and concern – that empathy can be utilized as a force for good. For we can experience difference and, rather than a sense of tolerance, feel hatred. Barack Obama has described how we suffer from an 'empathy deficit' in the modern world. Perhaps that's linked to our difficulty with mourning.

The ability to form communities is something to do with it too. If the basic unit of community is the family, then forming new families necessitates leaving old families, the one we grew up in. Hence, in the old wedding services, the father would give away – give up, lose – his daughter, so that she might form a new family. The action is a kind of mourning. The notion of a man giving a woman away is awkward now, because we realize that the notion of a man owning a woman is repellent. But there's something in the moment that's very powerful and moving, which perhaps explains why, against their rational selves, many women still want their fathers, or someone, to give them away at their wedding. It's a life-giving rite of mourning.

How to learn how to mourn? How to learn how to embrace loss so as to be able better to embrace life? I think it can be done in little ways, the ways that familiarize us with the losses that colour life. Again, my sense is that our ancestors did this quite naturally, and in all kinds of unexpected places. I do not know who first thought to demonstrate a logical syllogism with the equation, 'All men are mortal – Socrates is a man – Socrates is mortal.' But it is not just an example of logic, it is also a little exercise in mourning, in recognizing loss. Socrates was mortal.

Klein's advice might be consciously to give life a twist of death, like a twist of lemon in a drink. Not too much, and it actually enhances life's savour. When you go for a walk, try a walk in a cemetery. They can be very beautiful. When you chose a DVD or book, pick one that's a story about loss. They are common today, as in 'mis lit' or misery literature: there's a wisdom in the growth of the genre, a rebellion against the loss of loss in life. Or allow yourself time to be alone, time to be without others. This is solitude, which is different from loneliness, and is another meditation on loss. And if Klein is right, it's not the negation of love, but its precondition. For loving well, like living well, means being able to lose and to count the cost. It's when we don't allow ourselves to mourn that we slip into depression.

18

Music – and learning from mistakes

IT has long been noted that music has an extraordinary capacity to move us. Tears will well up in the eyes, or a smile creep across a face, at the sound of a few well struck notes. Melody and harmony appear to speak directly to our souls. Francis Bacon, the Elizabethan essayist, wrote that if he could devise a means of hearing music throughout the day, he would be sure he had reached heaven. So here we are.

Research suggests that our hominid ancestors communicated by means of musical sounds before they learned to speak words. Young babies have an innate and extraordinary capacity to distinguish between subtly different phonics. But there's something else that I want to pick up on about music here, because of what it suggests about the art of living. It stems from observations made by the philosopher Karl Popper.

Karl Popper (1902–94)

Quick summary: Popper is in contention for the title of greatest philosopher of the twentieth century, not least for his ideas about science and what he called the 'open society', one in which ideas are routinely and thoroughly tried in the court of public opinion.

Key text: His autobiography, entitled *Unended Quest* (1976), provides a great introduction to many of his biggest ideas.

Interesting fact: Karl Popper taught the wealthy financier George Soros, who develops his ideas in philanthropic work.

. . . .

> *'Extraordinary how potent cheap music is.'*
> Noël Coward

Mistakes and discords

Music was a dominant theme in Karl Popper's life. He remembered his mother playing the piano beautifully, and he wondered why it is often said that a family is 'musical', as his was. It can't be passed on genetically, as pianos, violins and European music in general have existed only for an instant in evolutionary terms. At one point he thought about pursuing music professionally and he even won a place in a conservatoire on account of a fugue he'd composed. But then he became more interested in the history of music.

One problem he puzzled over was this. Polyphony is peculiar to Western civilization. Counterpoint and harmony are European inventions. So what can be said about this 'miracle of the West'?

He made a study of the emergence of counterpoint out of the older practice of singing melodies in parallel octaves, fifths, and then thirds and fifths. It's this pattern that is the hallmark of the open, contemplative music we now associate with the early music period. This plainsong became more complicated when choirs began to sing not in parallel voices but by putting notes against notes. One would rise, while another fell. Fifths and fourths in the bass could fall, while tones and semitones in the treble rose. Perhaps this occurred first by accident, while rehearsing. 'It may have been an unintended result of a religious practice, namely the intoning of responses by the congregation,' Popper writes, making what was to be an important point for his theory. 'Mistakes of this kind in the singing of congregations are bound to occur.' But though a mistake, the new sound was pleasing. It delivered a sense of resolution. We now call them cadences. Out of a mistake, harmony was born.

Then came polyphony proper, the trick of writing all the different voices as if they were independent, each performing their own melody. Only they are united in their difference, and that combination of concord and discord yields the stirring sounds that composers like J. S. Bach brought to perfection. So to mistakes Popper added discord, as he searched for the origins of Western music. The two together seemed to be important.

Figure 18
Four Couples Dancing by Hartmann Schedel (1440–1514). Musicians portrayed in the *Nuremberg Chronicle*.

Traditions and restrictions

However, Popper also noted something else. The invention of music was not a free-for-all of mistakes and discords. For one thing, the church canonized certain melodies and controlled what could be sung in churches by dogmatic restrictions. But this is not a predicament to be lamented. 'It was the established *cantus firmus* which provided the framework, the order, the regularity that made possible inventive freedom without chaos,' he wrote in his autobiography. For it's the juxtaposition of the two, the correct notes and the mistakes, the concord and the discord, that creates the effect. There needs to be a ground base of tradition, upon which the new sounds can improvise, in order for a new cosmos of music to arise. It's old and new together that create the best compositions. Repress the novelty and you have stasis. Completely overthrow the strict conventions and you have cacophony not polyphony.

I learned as much when after many years of lessons on how to play classical music I took jazz improvisation classes. I wanted to be free of sheet music, and imagined that the free flow of jazz would be infinitely more expressive. But what I was taught came as a shock. Learning jazz required me to do far more practice at scales and arpeggios than I'd ever done before. My jazz teacher would sometimes make me do nothing but run up and down the keyboard for an entire half-hour. My hands had to learn the shape of the basic chords, across all combinations of keys. Perversely, perhaps, I learned far more about traditional harmony learning to improvise than I ever learned playing Widor or Chopin.

The reason, though, became clear. It is not until you have mastered the tradition, until you have learned to appreciate its richness and depth, that you can begin to make convincing improvisations of your own. Powerful discords are much more intimately linked to pleasing concord than I realized. Tension requires resolution and syncopation follows the beat, as much as melodies need silence. As Popper put it in his autobiography: 'The dogma provides us with the frame of coordinates needed for exploring the order of this new unknown and possibly in itself even somewhat chaotic world, and also for creating order where order is missing.'

> *'In the course of my life I have often had intimations in dreams that I should make music.'*
> Socrates

Originality and greatness

What this implies about the art of living is clear. We need our traditions. We should nurture them. And yet, tradition has become a bad word. Religious traditions carry a perception of oppression. Dogma is dictatorial. Other traditions in art and thought are treated warily in the modern world too. We prefer to chose a lifestyle, pick and mix from the options in the marketplace of ideas, follow fashions rather than make commitments. It's clear why: we value freedom and the sense of individual expression it brings. But there's a risk here, for, while freedom is undoubtedly a great good, freedom must be *for* something.

Think of it this way by reflecting on the love of novelty in the modern world. Newness alone is taken to be synonymous with creativity (mistakenly if Popper is right), and similarly, in the art of living, new experience is frequently posited as the path to freedom. But Popper points out that pure originality is not the most common ingredient in great works of music. And it is certainly the case that great musicians did not compose merely to display originality. 'The main aim of the true artist is the perfection of his work,' Popper writes. 'In a great work of art the artist does not try to impose his little personal ambitions on the work but uses them to *serve* the work. In this way he may grow, as a person, through interaction with what he does.'

Fitness and balance

In truth, though, it's the feedback between the artist and the traditions within which he or she is working that make for greatness. It's a dialogue with the tradition that's important, which means that the great artist must be fluent in the language of the tradition. Their freedom is found in their commitment to that language.

And yet, the tradition is not revered for its own sake, but because it provides rich resources for living. What's required is the right balance, a sense of the fit of the tradition with the life sought. That, too, requires training. If the youthful temperament has a tendency to rebel, and define itself *against* tradition, a more mature approach is able to value tradition, and make it work *for* you.

Tradition trouble

There is, then, this tension inherent in our relationship to traditions: Does a tradition serve us, or do we serve the tradition? Popper thought that Bach got it about right. 'Bach forgets himself in his work, he is a servant of his work,' Popper thought. 'Of course, he cannot fail to impress his personality upon it; this is unavoidable. But he is not, as Beethoven is, at times, conscious of expressing himself and even his moods.' Bach's workshop provides a model of learning. The musician learns by example, and also learns to grow up. Popper describes it in this way:

'[The individual] learns a discipline, but he is also encouraged to use his own musical ideas and he is shown how they can be worked out clearly and skilfully. His ideas may develop, no doubt. Through work the musician may, like a scientist, learn by trial and error. And with the growth of his work his musical judgement and taste may also grow – and perhaps even his creative imagination. But this growth will depend on effort, industry, dedication to his work; on sensitivity to the work of others, and on self-criticism. There will be a constant give and take between the artist and his work rather than a one-sided 'give' – a mere expression of his personality in his work.'

Substitute 'work' for 'life' in that paragraph, and put 'musical' in brackets, and the analogue with the art of living is clear.

A Step

There are a number of key elements, then, in the description Popper offers of the art of living. The individual must make good mistakes, and creative discord, but the 'good' and 'creative' here demand an immersion in a tradition, one that provides a framework for exploration and means that choice does not descend into chaos. Originality is not as important as the effort to perfect the work called life, and, if Bach is a good example, this means seeing your efforts as in the service of something greater than the efforts themselves. If trial and error is important, so is an ability to take critique. It's in the give-and-take between the new and old that great music emerges. So too with life.

A sense of that dialogue can be gleaned by imagining that you're going to design something, perhaps an item of clothing, or a kitchen, or a garden. Immediately, you've two options. One is to take a blank piece of paper and start from scratch. The chances are that the design won't be very good, and the effort will lead you to give up. The other option is to put the blank piece of paper to one side, and turn instead to previous designs, older designs, designs that can be said to work. From them, you may gain ideas of your own, perhaps the best being the result of unwitting mistakes, of pleasing discords. You'll be in good company, alongside the originators of polyphony who sang the wrong notes as they rehearsed the plainsong.

19

Pets – and the value of strangers

PEOPLE keep pets for as many reasons as the pets they have – dogs for company, parrots for entertainment, fish for relaxation, horses for exercise. Name an animal and owners will describe to you the specific delight they find in them. It's not just that our lives are intimately bound up with pets, and have been for millennia, ever since human beings first domesticated animals for food, transport and protection. More interesting, philosophically, is how our company with them tells us much about ourselves. Pets, I want to suggest, are enormously valuable when it comes to the art of living.

Michel de Montaigne (1533–92)

Quick summary: Montaigne was a French nobleman who, perhaps as a result of his odd childhood (he was bought up speaking only Latin), or as a result of his adult experience (he witnessed the untimely deaths of his best friend, child and had a near-death experience himself), retired early from public life to write reflective essays on life.

Key text: The *Essays* themselves are a ragbag of memoir, philosophy, history and entertainment, in which readers have persistently found they meet the man and then themselves.

> *'I am fond of pigs. Dogs look up to us. Cats look down on us. Pigs treat us as equals.'*
> Winston Churchill

Playing with cats

For myself, it's cats. Unlike dogs, which are all too human, cats force us to take up a different perspective on life. It was perhaps for the same reason that the Egyptians worshiped them, because they represent that which causes us confusion. It's been said they are the philosophical pet, and certainly they are creatures that preoccupied at least one philosopher, Michel de Montaigne.

The Renaissance essayist famously asked whether his cat was playing with him more than he was playing with his cat. 'We entertain each other with reciprocal monkey tricks,' he wrote. 'If I have my time to begin or to refuse, so has she hers.' It sparked a whole series of thoughts about life that became part of his longest essay. He liked cats because they are mysterious, they resist human control. That fitted with his quizzical approach to

Figure 19 The ancient Egyptians kept cats too.

life. 'We have some mediocre understanding of their meaning; so do they of ours, in about the same degree. They flatter us, threaten us, and implore us, and we them.'

And it's that confusion which I think can be so illuminating for us. I have two cats, Mandalay and Bhamo – named after two cities in Burma for they belong to that particularly sociable breed, the Burmese. I've been watching them. And they've led me to a number of reflections.

How they're like us

What particularly fascinates me about pets is the extent to which they are like us, and the moments we realize they are not. I sometimes wonder which of the attributes that humans have, and which might be said to make us human, do my cats also display. First, here are four which I suspect they do have:

1 The first attribute is **reason**. Now, clearly my cats don't do logic. Not even the keenest cat lover could claim that. But if reasoning is, in part, working something out by deduction, and not say by trial and error, I think that at least the smarter of my two felines has it to a degree.

    My evidence is a game they play, chasing each other around a table. The dumber one, Bhamo, always runs in just one direction. The smarter one, Mandalay, will double back and catch Bhamo out. It's the fact that one does and the other doesn't that makes me wonder whether Mandalay has powers of reason. I conclude that she has deduced something about how to win the game.

2 But what of **play** itself, Montaigne's famous reflection? Clearly, I think they do play. My evidence is toy mice. When Mandalay, say, brings in a real rodent she drops it and then leaves me to it, as a gift. But when she's playing with a toy mouse, she brings it to me, drops it – and wants me to throw it for her, much as a dog does

with a stick. I conclude that she knows the difference between a kill and a game.

3   All this playing is fun and very cute. But it raises a third question. Do the cats show me real **affection**? Or do they cuddle up to us just for the warmth, or in the hope of food? I conclude it's real affection, not only because I cannot bear to think of it otherwise, but because they will greet me and nuzzle up, far more than is necessary to deliver mere comfort. Also, I don't think it's my fantasy when I notice that they are especially affectionate when we've been away, much as we humans too want to spend time with those we're close to when we've not seen them for a while.

4   But that raises another, deeper question. Philosophers call it **theory of mind**, and it's to ask whether cats can attribute beliefs and desires to others and understand that those beliefs and desires are different from their own? At least in part, I think the answer must be yes too. The evidence is that Mandalay again (she is the smart one) will often sit looking at me. When I turn to look at her, our eyes will meet, and she will give a little miaow. Cute, again. But also, I think, she sees affection from me in the look we exchange.

Alternatively, she will play peek-a-boo, much like a child. If you hide your eyes behind your hand, she will move her head so as to re-establish eye contact. And it can become a game, because she will then lower her head so as to hide her eyes – waiting for me to eyeball her once more. That eye contact is highly significant. It suggests that she can attribute a mental state to me apart from her own.

How they're not like us

So much for the similarities. But what of the differences – and the confusion. The most obvious are to do with their attitudes towards smell and pain.

I remember the time one of them had a stinking ear infection. I caught the first sweet whiff of it at the weekend. By Tuesday it was strong enough to churn my stomach, and I thought I'd spotted the source, a mouldy glob, which I cleaned off. Wednesday, though, the smell was richer. So Thursday, I went to the vet, and Friday morning the cat was in again, to have the ear cleaned out. The vet spoke of black ooze as thick as mud, though her bloods were normal, and told me that, with luck, a course of antibiotics would quash it.

The pain must have been considerable. A child with an ear infection weeps all night; an adult groans. The cat showed no sign of it, her behaviour revealing not a moment's misery. I've heard it said that cats are brave: evolution has taught them not to show weakness, for only the fit survive. Once, one of my cats had a wound, a slice in the skin that was deep enough to reveal the muscle flexing beneath. The cat licked it, but still leapt on to chairs and tables. What feline skill enables them to tolerate and hide the pain? It's a capacity most humans do not have.

There are other ways in which cats *must* differ. One is that of empathy. This is not just the ability to recognize another consciousness, as the game of peek-a-boo implies, but is the further capacity imaginatively to enter into another creature's feelings in such a way that it leads to a costly change in their own action. The reason I think cats don't do empathy, or at least not much, is the habit they have of killing other creatures. When a bird is screaming in your mouth, or a mouse bleeding in front of you, and you carry on impassively, I don't think you can understand empathy.

Similarly, I don't think they do disgust. Their preferred place for a dead rat is not down the toilet, but in their mouth. They will quite happily lick faeces clinging to their behind. I can't think of one thing that my cats don't do that can be attributed to disgust. Some say cats steer clear of other cats who are dying. When our last cat died, there was no evidence of that from the others.

And here's a quality that they say dogs do have, but I

suspect cats don't. Once, I remember telling off my dog quite fiercely. She went to her basket – and then stayed there until, quite some time later, I remembered and went to forgive her. She felt shame. I've never noticed a cat behave like that. They will take a telling off but never appear downcast as a result.

> 'I'm not over-fond of animals. I am merely astounded by them.'
> David Attenborough

Pets and death

The confusion that pets, and my cats in particular, provoke is the main reason they can serve us well in life. To think about them is to receive a kind of training in life's quandaries. (And we think our job is to train *them*!) Nowhere is this truer than when it comes to the deepest of life's perplexities, death.

I confess that I worry, sometimes to excess, about the death of the cats – particularly Mandalay, for she is the inquisitive one, the one who needs nine lives in order to stay alive. She's just a cat, someone might say. To worry about pets is excessive. Well, yes. But that, again, is why they are so illuminating.

What do I learn from the worry? My fear is that she will be killed by a car, as I live by a busy road; or stolen by a neighbour, as she is beautiful to look at and I live in a built-up area. These are fears not without some justification. But there's more going on, I suspect. For the high likelihood is that she will die before I do. So I can also be sure that in the easily conceivable future I will have to face her death.

What, I've come to realize is that my excessive concern with my cat's death, as opposed, say, to my partner's death or my own, stems from the fact that my cat's death is one that I will be able to cope with. When it comes, it will hurt badly. But I also know I will recover from it. I don't know if I will recover from my partner's death, if I don't go first. And clearly I won't recover from my own.

So my excessive concern about my cat's death stems from the fact that it is the death of a creature I love that is nonetheless thinkable to me. Unlike the other deaths I will have to face, the cat's is a safe death to contemplate. When I look at her, I can just about manage to stare life's fragility in the face. It's something else that pets give: a sense of the tremendous value of life.

A Step

So the suggestion from these reflections is straightforward enough. If you don't have one, think about getting a pet. If you do have one, explore what they tell you about life!

20

Religion – and filling the God-shaped hole

RELIGION is never far from discussions about morality, whether you like it or not. The good life has been associated with the godly life for so long that we just can't ignore matters of belief, no matter how much we might wish we could. Of course, we now live in an age in which it is blindingly obvious that you can be 'good without God'. Few believe that everything and anything is permitted for atheists. There are some things that are unconditional for human beings, and you only have to be a human being to know that: the life of a child, the love of another, the veneration of the dead.

And yet there is something more profound and interesting to tease out here. Religion has, for most of human history, been the source of the stories that best speak to our moral sensibilities, that tell us what living well can mean. Hence, in the West, we aim to suffer little children, care for the widow, be good Samaritans, turn the other cheek, go the extra mile. As Graham Greene put it, when we think, say, of what betrayal means, we can't but help have in the back of our collective mind the story of Jesus' betrayal in the Garden of Gethsemane. (If you want to hear the same sentiment from an atheist, I can direct you to the French anarchist Pierre-Joseph Proudhon who remarked that to talk of what's right is to be condemned implicitly to deploy the language of religion.)

It's where we've come from. We just find ourselves using the metaphors of religion, and adopting its moral imperatives, even despite ourselves. Like the music of Bach, or the arches of Chartres Cathedral, it's a symbolic language that is too rich to ignore. It would be philistine (there I go again) to refuse such assets on the grounds that you don't believe. To do so would be reductive of your humanity.

If that's right, then something else follows: we can enrich our lives by tending to these stories, by caring about that tradition. Philip Pullman, the novelist who is sharply critical of organized religion, thought as much when he retold the Christian story in *The Good Man Jesus and the Scoundrel Christ* (2010). On the back cover of the book is inscribed, in bold gold letters, 'This is a Story'. It's a resonant phrase because Pullman, one of the master storytellers of our times, knows that stories matter immensely. He surely put his time and talent into this work, not to endorse any orthodox view, but to keep the story alive.

There's something else that suggests we should care about the link between religion and morality, for all that it's tricky. And I think this goes to the heart of the matter. We are restless creatures. We long for more. We can't help but sense that our lives are *for* something. Just what that something might be is the big question of our times. We might conclude that our lives are for our family; for the oppressed; for the pursuit of fame, money or power; for the pursuit of happiness.

For many, though, that restlessness is directed at what is variously called the transcendent, the spiritual, the good – the 'God-shaped hole'. Aristotle caught the sentiment when, in his book about ethics, the *Nicomachean Ethics*, he concluded:

'We must not heed those who advise us to think as human beings since we are human and to think mortal things since we are mortal, but we must be like immortals insofar as possible and do everything toward living in accordance with the best thing in us.' There's a paradox in being human. Although we are mortals, we long for intimations of immortality – in art, in love, in science, in religion. Aristotle's thought is that, unless we recognize that, our taste for immortality will be perverted. In particular, he worried, we'll seek the immortality of the tyrant – the bully, bureaucrat or dictator who seeks to live for ever by impressing their will on those around them.

So what are we to do about this predicament, we who live in a secular age? I'd suggest we wind the clock back to the start of the twentieth century, when this issue really began to take hold, and consider the reflections of an earlier soul, Bertrand Russell.

> *'We have just enough religion to make us hate,*
> *but not enough to makes us love one another.'*
> Jonathan Swift

Bertrand Russell (1872–1970)

Quick summary: Russell's life as a philosopher can be divided into two halves. The first was spent trying to show that mathematics is a self-contained system of truths. He failed in that, and so in the second half devoted his considerable energies and learning to writing, activism and education.

Key text: His *History of Western Philosophy* (1945) is a tremendous read. For his religious views, there's an excellent selection, edited by Louis Greenspan and Stefan Andersson, entitled *Russell on Religion* (1999).

Interesting fact: When he was imprisoned for his pacifist activities in 1918, Russell was asked what his religion was. He was amused that the prison officer who asked did not know how to spell his reply: agnostic.

Against religion

Russell is well known now for his anti-religious polemic. The lecture, later published as a book, *Why I Am Not a Christian*, marked a seminal moment in the history of twentieth-century secular humanism. There he explains why he doesn't believe in things like immortality. Dismissing life after death, he declared: 'I never like to think that after I am dead I shall be at the beck and call of silly mediums, and be obliged to utter whatever may appear to them to be words of wisdom.' He objects to the biblical records in which Jesus is portrayed as coming to bring judgment, for their repellent and intolerant tone. What kind of monster would condemn even monsters to eternal torture and punishment?

In *Why I Am Not a Christian* Russell reserves special loathing for organized religion, which he believes rests on the cultivation of fear, the fear of what comes next. To play on people's concerns about death is, he concludes, cruel and undermines human happiness. He also believes that the intransigent commitment that people have to their religious beliefs has made for much that is evil in the world, not least wars.

He expresses a kind of secular courage, which is attractive: 'We ought to stand up and look the world frankly in the face. We ought to make the best we can of the world, and if it is not so good as we wish, after all it will still be better than what these others have made of it in all these ages. A good world needs knowledge, kindliness, and courage; it does not need a regretful hankering after the past or a fettering of the free

Figure 20 Bertrand Russell

intelligence by the words uttered long ago by ignorant men. It needs a fearless outlook and a free intelligence. It needs hope for the future. . .'

The eternity of maths

However, there is more to Russell on religion than perhaps meets the eye. For one thing, he was ever conscious of the limits of human understanding and the boundaries of certainty. Earlier he had written what he called a 'Liberal Decalogue', a secular version of the Ten Commandments, and the first commandment was this: 'Do not feel absolutely certain of anything.' That cuts both ways. Don't feel certain of God, but don't feel so certain about being an atheist too. He also liked to tease people about his beliefs. He once told a journalist who asked him about his dedication to humanity that: 'I think, on the whole, that the non-human part of the cosmos is much more interesting and satisfactory than the human part.'

There is a sense, in fact, in which you can say that Russell *was* religious. He was certainly not religious in the sense of signing up to the creeds of a church. His grandmother was a stern and dogmatic believer, and he clearly rejected that approach. But he inherited, nonetheless, what the theologian Friedrich Schleiermacher called 'a sense and taste for the infinite'.

This is what appealed to him about mathematics. As a young person he discovered Euclid's axioms, the foundations of geometry that are apparently timeless truths. That discovery can be described as a kind of religious awakening, though he longed to prove the axioms, rather than assume that they're true, as mathematicians before him had done. This launched him on his great mathematical quest: he sought a foundation for mathematics that doesn't rest on what is unproven.

He began full of Platonic hope, in the hope of discovering a mathematical world that was a realm of changeless eternity. However, after many years' struggle, the quest ended when those 'religious' hopes were dashed. It was like a loss of faith.

He never recovered from it. And when, in the later part of his life, a younger and as brilliant mathematician, Kurt Gödel, showed that every mathematical system of any complexity must have elements within it that can't be proven, Russell remained disillusioned.

Religious sensibilities

It's not surprising then that, after Russell's death, his daughter wrote that her father had been a religious man. He knew about religious experiences too, which he called 'mystic illumination'. When the wife of his close collaborator A. N. Whitehead almost died, Russell was deeply moved, perhaps in part because he was in love with her. But he records how, at that time, he was able to stare pain in the face and it provoked in him a new compassion for the world around him. He also wrote a mystical novel, though, to be frank, it's not very good.

He brings his various experiences and searches together in an essay, 'The Essence of Religion'. It's a fascinating counterpoint to *Why I Am Not a Christian*. In it, he advocates a religious sensibility without dogma. He writes:

'Acts inspired by religion have some quality of infinity in them: they seem done in obedience to a command, and though they may achieve great ends, yet it is no clear knowledge of these ends that makes them seem imperative. The beliefs which underlie such acts are often so deep and so instinctive as to remain unknown to those whose lives are built upon them. Indeed, it may be not belief but feeling that makes religion: a feeling which, when brought into the sphere of belief, may involve the conviction that this or that is good, but may, if it remains untouched by intellect, be only a feeling and yet be dominant in action. It is the quality of infinity that makes religion, the selfless, untrammelled life in the whole which frees men from the prison-house of eager wishes and little thoughts.'

There's a number of reflections in this paragraph which capture some of the links between religious feelings and what's good. Moral concerns have a 'quality of infinity' in them, which is to say that they must feel irresistible to us, for all that we fail to live up to them. The theologian Paul Tillich used the phrase 'ultimate concerns'. Ethics also comes from a place that is deep and instinctive, more a feeling than a belief. They speak from a profound part of our humanity, and that's why to follow them expands our humanity. What the good life achieves above all is freeing us from 'the prison house' of our petty worries, from the selfish thoughts that would make tyrants of us all.

> 'My country is the world, and my religion is to do good.'
> Thomas Paine

Man for our times

Russell, then, is so interesting in this debate because he embodied so many of the tensions we face today when working out how religion connects to morality. He did reject religion, when it came to dogma and the Church. He believed quite strongly that human beings can pursue happiness without God, and certainly that individuals can be good without God, not least because religious creeds can turn decent folk into monsters. In his activism, he often saw religion as the enemy because it constrained and limited human freedom.

However, he could not quite put the religious instinct, the sense and taste for the infinite, to one side. It inspired him too. This agnosticism deepened his moral life, inspiring a universal feeling of good and compassion. It helped him escape the prison-house of the self, by offering an impartial, infinite perspective. He recognized that it is often religious convictions that lead people to great acts of charity and self-sacrifice. There's something going on in religious traditions, he might have argued, that for all the concerns, is very valuable when it comes to living life to the full.

A Step

There is no easy resolution to these tensions. If anything, today we are even more aware of them than Russell was, though perhaps we shouldn't be so surprised at that. If religious feelings speak of our restless humanity, then it's a restlessness that can clearly be demonic as well as saintly. It can make tyrants of us as well as lovers. It might only be expected that religion has these demonic and saintly sides too. The solution, though, would not be to throw religion out, for, with the bathwater of dogmatism, you risk discarding the baby of inspiration too, that tremendous source of moral seriousness.

Better to be honest, like Russell. If you don't sense the 'quality of infinity', fair enough. If you do, then it might offer you 'the gift of a fresh eye and an untrammelled curiosity,' as Russell put it elsewhere.

Next time you are reflecting upon the timelessness of Euclid's axioms, are in a cathedral with soaring arches, or hear some astonishing religious music, you might like to ask how they speak to you of what's unconditionally good.

21

Responsibility – or what you would die for

THERE *is a worry that bothers nearly all contemporary discussions about ethics and how to live, and so we must find a space to discuss it here. It's one that's emerged and grown because we now live in a plural culture. It can be put very simply: what is true?*

It matters because if there is no basis for our morality, no such thing as meaning in life, nothing other than ourselves against which to orient ourselves, then there's effectively no good life to seek. We can just make it up. What doesn't work today, we can discard tomorrow – after all every life would be as good, or bad, as any other.

This chopping and changing is called *moral relativism*. It's a worry as it seems to imply that it's hard, if not impossible, to work out what we should do. If there's nothing that can be said to be good or bad, nothing that's worth living for, let alone worth dying for, then the art of living is for nought – or at least life is really the art of living on the edge of the abyss.

Some philosophers have concluded that is, in fact, about right. But one who didn't, while not denying the challenge of relativism, was Søren Kierkegaard. His answer, in a word, was responsibility. We – you and I – must take responsibility for our lives. We must find the way of life that is true for us.

> *'Values are tapes we play on the Walkman of the mind: any tune we choose so long as it does not disturb others.'*
> Jonathan Sacks

Søren Kierkegaard (1813–55)

Quick summary: Kierkegaard was a Danish writer whose work eventually gave rise to the philosophy of existentialism. He is remembered particularly for his profound moral insights.

Key text: One of his most important texts is *Fear and Trembling* in which he considers the famous story of Abraham and Isaac in the Hebrew Bible.

Interesting fact: He is sometimes remembered as a Christian philosopher too, and for the phrase a 'leap of faith'. He believed he was not a Christian but was trying to make that leap to become one.

The value of the subjective

Kierkegaard believed that the most important kind of truth, when it comes to how we should live, is not actually *objective* truth, the kind which is under threat from relativism.

The Death of *Socrates* (1787) by Jacques-Louis David. Socrates was one person who, for Kierkegaard, demonstrated that there was something for which he was prepared to sacrifice all.

It is, rather, *subjective* truth: is it true for me? Kierkegaard articulated it this way: 'The thing is to find a truth which is truth for me, to find the idea for which I am willing to live and die.' He continues: 'Certainly I won't deny that I still accept an imperative of knowledge, and that one can also be influenced by it, but then it must be taken up alive in me, and this is what I now see as the main point. . .'

His point is that moral knowledge, the kind that we live by, is not like scientific knowledge. Scientific knowledge is like water, which can be poured from one vessel into another. Like the water in your glass, it is objective – out there – and so can be stored and accumulated over time. But moral knowledge is different. It is shaped and forged by living traditions. And so while it exists over time, it must emerge from, and merge with, the life of communities and individuals – that is, be written in their life, taken up alive in me.

Against relativism

'What is true for me' might sound like just another version of relativism. After all, what's true for you may be different, so how are we to tell what's better, if not best? But Kierkegaard is not advocating holding to whatever pops into your head. And he's not saying we can't have an argument about why I might be wrong and you might be right. He is arguing that what's true is found in the lives we actually lead. We can tell what's best by the people we become. By their fruits you shall know them.

He worried that human beings, in the modern world, enamoured by intellectual systems and empirical science, were developing a marked tendency to hold back from life. They resisted plunging into the messiness of existence, with its confusions of right and wrong, in preference for an apparently impartial perspective that could tell what was good without being soiled by any of the mess. What he noticed is that this objective viewpoint requires you to be distant from life. It's a view from nowhere, which means that it is detached from what actually lives. Follow that advice, and you become a spectator of life not a participant in it. It privileges the opinion of the person who is out of it, over the experience of the person who's been through it. But ask yourself, Kierkegaard implies, who would you prefer as a guide? The individual alongside you, or the authority aloof and above you?

> 'Waste no more time arguing what a good man should be. Be one.'
>
> Marcus Aurelius

The art of living

The truth that is true for me is, then, not whimsical or arbitrary. It is not the case that anything will do. Rather, it is that which I can resolve to commit to. And that's the truth that, if I can live up to it, will transform my life. There is good reason to value objective truth in other kinds of contexts – if you're a mathematician, if you're an economist. But if it's life you're after, then objectivity offers you remarkably little. You can pay lip service to it. You can recite its creeds. But its a kind of truth that can't live in you. Only the imperatives that carry the force of being true for you are worth following.

The truth of that can be felt by considering some of the other issues we're considering in this book. Which of them is best assessed by asking whether they are objectively true? Is forgiveness, or mourning, or gratitude? Or which of them can be tested in a lab? Can beauty, or wonder, or music? Science can tell us a little about them. It can provide a few pointers. But unless they become part of a practice, they remain as dead as an equation, as lifeless as a cut of meat. Kierkegaard is not interested in discrediting science, but he does realize that whether or not a scientific result is true is another of these objective questions – interesting, for sure, but not enough to live by. In his notebooks, he reflects back on a time when he too turned to the sciences for all the answers. He wrote:

'That's what I lacked for leading a completely human life and not just a life of knowledge, to avoid basing my mind's development on – yes, on something that people call objective – something which at any rate isn't my own, and base it instead on something which is bound up with the deepest roots of my existence, through which I am as it were grown into the divine and cling fast to it even though the whole world falls apart. This, you see, is what I need, and this is what I strive for. . .'

The truth of forgiveness, mourning, gratitude; beauty, wonder and music must be pursued in a life, it must be acquired by you and I as persons. That is what we can argue about. How is it true for you; why is it true? Only the argument takes place in existential terms, via the stories I might tell you, the art we could make, and ultimately the fruits of our lives. We can study these things together – the nature of anger, the difference between us and the beasts, the rules of friendship. But they're arts, not strict sciences. They require us to talk about our take on them, and demand our powers of interpretation and discernment to tell us whether they're right.

Truth deniers

You can see Kierkegaard's point in a different way if you ask why human beings talk about moral truth at all. There are good reasons why we do, for the reason that it makes us responsible – not just to ourselves but to one another too. And that provokes certain consequences.

For example, being social animals means that we share our knowledge of the world, and that is a useful thing to do, as it enables us collectively to have access to more knowledge than we possibly could alone. Sharing knowledge instils certain virtues in us, notably accuracy and sincerity. To value accuracy is to value knowledge that, if true for you, is likely to have something to say to me if I can get it right. To value sincerity is to value the sharing of that knowledge in such a way that you are speaking honestly and subjectively, for that again is the kind of knowledge that will be most useful to me.

In other words, the concept of moral truth is deeply implicated in certain virtues that we value, and moreover we value those virtues because they seem part and parcel of a flourishing life. We can be responsible for them, simply by virtue of being committed to life. They are what make us what we've become and are becoming.

Subjective, but not private

But here's a further question to ponder. Even if moral truth is fundamentally subjective, because it is grounded in human lives, that doesn't mean it is just a private matter. Rather, it seems to one that we need to discuss widely with others. Consider this thought experiment.

Imagine making contact with intelligent life on another planet and having the wherewithal to communicate with the aliens. What would you choose to talk about?

An obvious option would be to discuss mathematics. It seems intuitively right to presume that the mathematics that works on planet Earth would also work elsewhere. A circle here would be a circle there. A quadratic equation here would describe the shape of a curve there too. That would initiate one line of exchange.

But say you then wanted to push the encounter in a different direction, and see what the extraterrestrials considered as good. Would you expect them to have moral concepts, a tradition about the art of living, just as the human species on planet Earth does? Just what counted as good or bad would presumably vary, as it does here, because the aliens would know what's true because it was true for them, just like us. But that wouldn't rule out the existence of alien moral philosophy, the discussion of good and bad per se.

Kierkegaard was fascinated by the small number of figures in history who he felt really embodied this moral insight, that they showed something was true because it was true for them. Abraham and Jesus were two, and another was Socrates. Socrates' moral responsibility showed nowhere more clearly than in the manner of his death.

Socrates is a particularly poignant example for two reasons. One is that he could easily have escaped from the prison in which he was being held, and so have avoided the hemlock that awaited him on the appointed day. Bribing guards was a fairly acceptable practice for aristocrats, or those with wealthy friends.

The other is that Socrates had spent his life walking around Athens declaring that there was one thing he knew for certain, that he knew nothing for sure. This is what made him a philosopher, a lover of, or seeker after, wisdom. So, you might ask, if he was uncertain about what is right, what is good, what is true, then why would he be prepared to die for it – for anything?

That Socrates was prepared to die for what he *believed* to be true, for all that it ultimately eluded him, was, though, precisely what drew Kierkegaard to him. There can be no greater expression of taking responsibility for your beliefs, for all the uncertainties, than that. So, it's the biggest question that Kierkegaard asks of us: What would you die for? If you can answer that, you know what is unconditionally true for you – and it's a gift that no science or creed alone can give you.

22

Seeing – a lesson in looking at the world

SEEING is *different from hearing, smelling and tasting. Whereas ears, noses and tongues are essentially passive sense organs, the eyes are active. For sure, light comes into the pupil, hits the retina, fires the optic nerve and ignites the brain. But our eyes also gaze out at the world. How we look at others affects how we see them. Sight gives as well as receives.*

A look can be intimidating or inviting, withering or welcoming. You can caress with your eyes, and curse with them. One can gaze aimlessly in a daydream, or one can observe carefully, pay attention, pass judgment. There are all kinds of things that can delight the eyes – shimmers of light, sunsets, a symphony of colours – but nothing is more satisfying than to behold the sight of another returning your look of love. Hence, when I look at the body of my beloved, I see another person, and so we can make love. But when I look at the body of a sexy stranger, I only see another body.

The word *egalitarian* literally means 'eye-level': in an egalitarian society everybody is able to look at everybody else with no gaze being inherently more advantageous than any other gaze. Or think of the word *pupil*. It comes from the Latin for 'doll' because when you look at someone, your pupil carries a diminutive, mirror reflection of them, as if they were a puppet in your eye – a person in your mind's eye. Or again, there is the familiar observation that people in traditional societies are wary of having their photograph taken, believing that the camera is a machine that can absorb power solely by its gaze.

So seeing is the moral sense. How we look at the world will affect how we live in the world. Seeing is something that we do, and we can do it in a good or a bad way. The individual who sees the world as a bad place will fear it. Someone who looks on what they survey as basically good will love the world as a result. We must think about our gaze as part of thinking about the good life.

> *'The ear receives, the eye looks. . . one can terrify with one's eyes not with one's ear or nose.'*
> Ludwig Wittgenstein

Jean-Paul Sartre (1905–80)

Quick summary: The most famous of the existentialist philosophers, Sartre believed to be human is to be radically free – so free, in fact, that it becomes a burden to us, leading to feelings of anxiety and dread.

Key text: *Being and Nothingness* (1943) is his major philosophical work, though it's not an easy read. *Existentialism Is a Humanism* (1946) provides an accessible introduction.

Interesting fact: Sartre was not only a philosopher, but a playwright, poet and novelist. He was offered the Nobel Prize for Literature in 1964, though he declined it.

What we intend

Jean-Paul Sartre is a philosopher who can help us with sight. It was of such interest to him because it is the sense that reveals something crucial about our consciousness. It is intentional. Consciousness and sight alike are always directed outwards and towards. The gaze reaches out from the eyes and seizes, holds or grazes the world – the different mood in our look depending on what we intend by our gaze.

Think of the way we imagine objects, Sartre suggested. Images are not like tiny photographs in our mind that we then match up with the objects that we see in the world. Sight is not a game like Snap. Rather, the image you have in your mind's eye is your creation. When you imagine your favourite food or place, you recall it exhibiting all its best features – the delicious aroma, the sunny view. You choose to assign it those features. There is much about choice in sight. (A corollary is that it's very hard to take a photograph of that place because a photograph can't convey what's in your mind's eye.)

A more disturbing side of the active nature of seeing emerges if you think about how we look at other people. It's governed, Sartre thought, by what can be called a master/slave relation. If I look at you, you are reduced to being an object in my field of view. This is why staring at someone is so offensive. It's a threat because it cuts them down to size. Hence, we tend not to look strangers in the eyes, and only stare at them if we think we will not be spotted.

The natural response if you do see someone looking at you is to stare back: you try to make me an object in your field of view – to cut me down to size, to control me, to 'hold me' in your gaze. Seeing is, therefore, a kind of power struggle. Were it not for the fact that our encounters with one another are embedded in all sorts of relationships – as citizens, as workmates, as friends, as fellow human beings – war might well be the natural consequence of the apparently simple act of looking at others. Again, seeing is a supremely ethical activity.

Custody of the eyes

For the ancient Greeks, sight was recognized as a moral concern. They were helped in this view by their understanding of the physics of light. The modern view is that light enters the eye. Rays of electromagnetic radiation, travelling in straight lines, bounce off the objects we see, and are focused by the eye's lens to form an inverted image on the retina. Modern optics therefore stresses a *passive* understanding of sight, which is perhaps why we don't think of it so much in moral terms now.

However, according to ancient optics, sight is possible because of the rays that the eye emits. The eyes act rather like searchlights, scanning the world as they move across things. Seeing is therefore *active* and willed. It is not just a question of what I do, but how I do it. Hence in Euclid, the physics of optics is linked to the moral use to which we put our eyes. From this, it follows that people can be trained to see well.

It's for the same reason that ancient books of spirituality always pay careful attention to sight. It was called *custodia oculorum*, or custody of the eyes. It's not just that the eyes must be guarded against seeing the wrong things – those things that might distract the individual from the pursuit of the good life. But also, that seeing is a habit which must be directed aright, for how you look at the world says much about who you are and what you're becoming.

Books of spiritual practice discussed how the eyes must be prevented from flitting from one thing to another, in constant search of distraction – a symptom, it was believed, of a distracted soul. Or they encouraged the individual to look on others as God looks on them, and as if other individuals were in fact divine themselves. Hence, the spiritual person has the habit of regarding the world as a gift, a blessing, a wonder. They look with the eyes of love.

The mystery of light

Sight was mysterious too, for the remarkable thing about seeing is that we don't actually see light itself, but rather the objects in our field of view. Shapes, colours and reflections are revealed by light. If we did see light itself, then we presumably wouldn't see anything else at all. To see light would be like staring into a luminescent fog. Paradoxically, it would be blinding.

The reason is that light is like the carrier wave of a radio signal. It must be present to see, but must be invisible in order to allow seeing. This means that it can be thought of as a metaphor for God: if God can be said to sustain the universe, then God would also have to be invisible in the universe. As God said to Moses, no one can see God and live. It's a bit like the notion of God as the ground of existence. If God is the ground of existence, then God cannot be said to exist. Neither can God be said *not* to exist. God, like light, is somehow beyond existence, beyond being seen, by virtue of being that which makes seeing possible.

That might seem esoteric, but perhaps not as much as the rather abstract passage above might suggest. One day I found myself sitting in an optician's chair, having a sight test. The optician shone a pencil-beam of bright light into my eye, and I almost had a religious experience. What happened was this: I saw my retina. It was reflected, presumably on the front of my eyeball, and so my retina had the odd experience of seeing itself, something it does not usually do. It looked like a map, painted in dense pinks, lined with a delicate filigree of grey-blue rivers.

The vision set me thinking. That we don't see our retinas is perhaps a bit like the fact that, when we think, we don't detect the workings of the brain's soft grey matter. The tissue, in some way, does the thinking. But no amount of introspection will, of itself, make us feel a neuron. It remains hidden. And that's rather like the relationship between seeing and light – and, indeed, between the believer and God.

> *'My gaze touches the place were you feel*
> *yourself to be.'*
> Raymond Tallis

Having a world view

The way we see the world also affects our possibilities
in life. It's called our 'world view', and it determines our
imagination and the choices that present themselves to us. It
refers to the frame through which we see things, and much like
a picture frame brings some options into focus while excluding
others.

Or you might say your world view is your theory of life,
as the word *theory* comes from the Greek for a 'look' or 'view'.
If you have the wrong theory, then you will never completely
grasp what's possible. Like a misguided scientist who will never
be able to make much sense of the evidence, have the wrong
world view and you will miss out on much in life. It's all a
question of how you see things, and seeing things differently
can be transformative.

This explains one of the reasons why parenting is so
important. Your parents shape the way you see the world. In
fact, it's possible to go a step further and say that how your
parents see the world is likely to determine how you do too,
because you watch them and so learn how to see things as
they do. Hence, children tend to do the same kind of jobs as
their parents. Professional parents have children who become
professionals. Parents who pursue vocations tend to have
children in vocational jobs too. Conversely, the child who
rebels against their parents might protest that their elders
have a blinkered view of the world. In their rebellion, they are
struggling to leave that way of seeing things behind – though,
more often than not, their very rebellion will be a reaction
against it and so still be framed by it. Hence, the politician's
child becomes an anarchist. The vicar's child becomes an
atheist.

Returning to Sartre, we find that his analysis encourages us to seize the freedom we have as individuals by focusing on *how we see things* – literally and metaphorically. The aim is to widen your scope and question the theories you have about life and the world. And there is no more practical and immediate way of doing so than to become more conscious of how you look at others – at those habits of sight that would welcome, condemn, enquire, love. Only then might you see things differently, and in so doing come to live a different, perhaps better life.

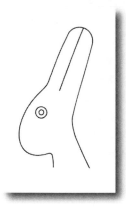

Figure 22 Is it a duck? Is it a rabbit?

Remember the duck–rabbit image? It's the drawing that can be seen both as a duck and as a rabbit, and will flip from one to the other as you look. It's so fascinating because it displays so vividly how seeing is an activity. *How* you look determines *what* you see. In the case of the duck–rabbit, what shifts is the representation of an animal. But when it comes to seeing and the good life, what shifts is your view of life as a whole. Look well to live well. At a material level nothing may change. And yet, at a moral level, everything can seem different.

23

Sex – and what makes it good

TODAY *we take it as read that human beings are sexual beings. Freud argued that sex is like hunger, needing to be sated, and ever since then sex has been thought of as a little like bread. Sometimes it's a quick slice of toast in the morning, to be snatched before you head out to work. Or it might be like lunchtime sandwiches, part of your staple diet, something you have three or four times a week. Sex, like bread, can become a little stale, even mouldy. At times, it can be combined with other ingredients – a candlelit dinner, expensive scent – to become the equivalent of an indulgent treat, like a bread-and-butter pudding. But it's still bread, what economists would call a commodity.*

And it's that commodification that is the aspect to be concerned about. It's not sex itself, but the use of sex to sell pretty much everything, or the sense in which our discourse about sex revolves around pleasure and performance. What's lost are the intangibles, particularly that a good relationship is the key to good sex, and that intimacy is about much more than treating the body as a love-machine. This is particularly apparent in the worries about keeping your sex life lively. We ask whether lovers, who have been together for some time, need to spice up their sex lives. Or whether it's time for a little experimentation, like purchasing a rye loaf for a change, or opting for something Italian.

But shouldn't we expect more from sex than the erotic equivalent of toast? Does our humanity actually long for what Christians do with bread, when they share it as a sacrament? For long-term lovers, their partner's body becomes an extension of their own. In the same way that they feel part of each other's lives – that the sense of who they are is intimately linked to the life of their partner – so sex becomes a reflection of this connection. Is there a dynamic we're missing then, in which the joy of physical closeness does not stand or fall on pleasure or performance, but on relationship? If the promise is good sex, it's surely worth asking about it.

> '[The question of sex] shrivels like a salted snail when compared to the towering question of love.'
> Stephen Fry

Martin Buber (1878–1965)

Quick summary: Informed by existentialist philosophy, and the idea that the challenge of life is to become a person, Buber proposed that relationship is a fundamental category in life, and that we relate to our fellows by encountering each other as I and Thou.

Key text: A number of his books are published as classics, including *I and Thou* (1923) and *Between Man and Man*.

Interesting fact: Buber was Jewish and fled the Nazis during the war, before settling in Palestine where he became a strong advocate of an Arab–Jewish state.

. . . .

I–Thou

Human relationship, for Buber, is an 'existential communication'. When we relate fully, we recognize the personhood in each other, and in so doing become persons ourselves. We know when it happens as we then have 'the experience of dialogue'.

Buber's point is that our relationships with other people are not like our relationships with other things: they are what he called 'I–Thou' relationships, not 'I–It'. Your relationships with things are largely instrumental. Is it working? Can I use it? Should I get a replacement? Do I need it? Things are what you go out and get. But a relationship with a person is different, and if you treat an I–Thou as an I–It, you kill the encounter stone dead – lovers treated as the service providers in your sex life. You can speak *about* things, but you speak *to* people and lovers.

If that's right, the problem with much of our discussion about sex is that it has forgotten that it is in relation to relationship that we should aspire to talk about it. That would be different from treating sex as an essentially biological activity, the kind that 'sexperts' fall back on when advising on the logistics. It is different from thinking of sex as an economic exchange, by which is meant not so much paying for sex, but treating sex as a transaction – as when it is suggested that you should discuss your sexual needs with your partner as if you were each participants in a supply chain. You're not; you're people in a human relationship, Buber would say. What you're handling here is an I–Thou relationship. It's an interaction, a dialogue – conducted in the language of intimacy, openness, reciprocity and commitment, as well as words. To be in a sexual relationship is not like going to the supermarket to acquire the bread for lunch.

Sex and love

What makes good sex good, and bad sex bad is whether it falls into the category of I–Thou or I–It. It-sex misuses a person, is dehumanizing. This would happen even if the other person consented to being treated as an object. The partners would then both be abusing themselves as persons. (Rape might be defined as It-sex that deliberately refuses the possibility of a Thou relationship. Hence its violence.)

A good sexual relationship is about the responsibility of one for another, when each aspires to treat the other as a

'Thou', for the other's sake, and indeed for their own – that they may be known as a 'Thou' too. Good sex also entails commitment for Buber, because to be persons ourselves we need to be committed to by others. We have a past and a future, not just a present, so when it aims to span time, sex is good because it aims to sustain a relationship.

There can be a substantial grey area between the two in, say, casual encounters, because, even when lust is in command, people can be extraordinarily generous to one another. We find it hard to treat each other as things. Similarly, it takes time to make commitments, and so the search for an I–Thou relationship does not preclude experiments that might, in practice, veer more towards the I–It. Mistakes are allowed. But the aim is enduring love, and a commitment that deepens with time. The intimacy shared by long-term loving partners will get better, even if the sexual acrobatics declines.

> 'The sexual world of the fantasist is a world without subjects, in which others appear as objects only.'
> Roger Scruton

On etchings

But do you buy it? Do you believe that good sex is about I–Thou relationships? Isn't there such a thing as 'just sex'?

I think Buber's thesis is proven by experience. The existence of fetishes suggests as much, a fetish being the tendency to ascribe personal qualities to impersonal things, chasing after an I–Thou relationship when it can only be an I–It. Or you might wonder why it's so hard to write about sexual relationships in a novel. The temptation that too many authors fall for is to describe the mechanics, and that reads comically because when we expect I–Thou, we find I–It.

But perhaps the most common demonstration stems from the way people use euphemisms when asking for sex, particularly when the relationship they seek with the person concerned makes the asking difficult or inappropriate. It's the 'Would you like to see my etchings?' tendency. The interesting question is why we resort to these circumlocutions, when it's quite clear that we are asking 'just for sex'? The reason would be that, even when we seek an encounter with no strings, implicitly we know there are strings – the strings arising from the fact that we are persons, not things.

What the euphemism does is allow the other party to forgive the dehumanizing request, given that they regard it as such. It means that they can hold on to a part of themselves where they aren't treated like an It. He or she can either pretend the request never occurred, or, in his or her response to the request, implicitly acknowledge the mistake of the other and indicate that it need not necessarily spoil the human relationship they have.

Such a generous response would be a moral action, one that restored the relationship to an I–Thou. It shows that this thing of immense worth, a human relationship, is at stake, and all for the sake of a good time. The euphemism helps in this, and is surely why we naturally deploy them: a direct request for sex would be much harder to forgive since the relationship issue would have to be confronted as bluntly as the request for sex itself was. In Buber's language: a euphemism keeps open the possibility of restoring to I–Thou what you've treated as I–It. In common language, 'Do you want to see my etchings? / No thanks' is a much easier exchange than 'Can I have sex with you? / No: and now, do you accept my forgiveness of you for asking?'

Try both options out. Before you've uttered the words, you'll know the difference.

Atomization and suicide

Buber was Jewish, and his notion of I–Thou relationships extends to the eternal I–Thou relationship that he envisaged with God. He calls an I–Thou relationship 'an instinct to make contact', and that includes cosmic as well as personal connections. Karl Marx, though an atheist, could argue similarly to Buber. Marx wrote:

'Love can only be exchanged for love, trust for trust, etc.. . . If you love without evoking love in return, i.e. if you are not able, by the manifestation of yourself as a loving person, to make yourself a beloved person, then your love is impotent and a misfortune.'

Marx wrote movingly about his relationship with his wife, describing how he found himself in her embrace and kisses. As Buber would have it, he knew himself as a Thou with his wife, and so became an I.

When that dialectic fails, the result is the dehumanization of the individuals concerned. It's a subject explored in the novels of the French writer Michel Houellebecq, which carry titles like Atomized. In Atomized, Houellebecq tells the story of two half-brothers, Michel and Bruno. Large sections of the book are taken up with Bruno's sexual exploits. He signs up for a holiday camp that encourages casual erotic adventures, and meets Christiane, a libertine. She introduces him to the joys of the 'orgy circuit'. The inability of casual sex to fulfil them as people becomes graphically clear when Christiane reveals that she suffers from a degenerative condition. It eventually confines her to a wheelchair, and, though they try to remain together, their love lacks the strength for it.

Houellebecq describes the moment this becomes clear. Christine is in her wheelchair. She moves towards Bruno, and although they kiss, they are not able to look each other in the eye – they are not able to hold each other's gaze.

According to Buber's analysis, their inability to share their gaze stems from the nature of their relationship: It is I–It not I–Thou. Buber wrote: 'He who loves a woman, and brings her life to present realization in his, is able to look in the Thou of her eyes, into a beam of the eternal Thou.' There is no such gazing in Houellebecq's novel. Christiane commits suicide. She fails to find herself as an I, lacking Thou relationships, and literally fails to live. Bruno doesn't kill himself, but ends up in a psychiatric ward, treated as an It by drugs and science.

For Houellebecq, sex is just a particularly intense point in life, which demonstrates that life, for many modern people, has become a question of pleasure, and little else besides. 'Each individual has a simple view of the future,' he writes: 'A time will come when the sum of pleasures that life has left to offer is outweighed by the sum of pain. . . This weighing up of pleasure and pain which, sooner or later, everyone is forced to make, leads logically, at a certain age, to suicide.' He describes a world in which we have become I–It to one another, and lost the capacity for the pleasure of the I–Thou.

Buber's invitation to have good sex can seem wildly idealistic, and possibly suspiciously moralistic. It is both. But a quick analysis of sexual experience will indicate, to most, that it is no less right.

Remember the last time you felt someone brushing your hand, making a sexual pass that was unwanted. Your reaction was to withdraw. The touch felt cold, unwelcome. Now remember the last time you felt your lover brushing your hand. Physically speaking, it's exactly the same touch, only this time you will have returned it, and the warmth.

The difference shows that sexual pleasure, for we humans, has everything to do with the personal nature of the encounter. The *who* matters as much as the *how*. We can find stimulation in I–It encounters. The existence of pornography is proof enough. But when you want to love a person, not just a body – which in Buber's scheme is to say, when you want to become a person too – sex must be the expression of an I–Thou relationship. You have to drop the I–It.

24
Stillness – its intensification of life

STILLNESS is quite a skill to master in a world that is constantly on the move. It's difficult literally to be still; only the dead truly manage it. And it's as difficult to attain an inner stillness, the two being intimately linked. It's a tricky concept for the Western mind too, as the good life for us is almost invariably about activity, about doing something. Flourishing implies doing, not letting be. Stillness looks like doing nothing, so how can that be part of an engaged life? And yet there's something in stillness that is definitely worth teasing out.

> 'We all have within us a centre of stillness surrounded by silence.'
> Dag Hammarskjöld

Lao Tzu
(sixth century BCE)

Quick summary: Taoism, with which Lao Tzu is associated, is a way of life that has been summarized as 'letting it be'. Attunement is valued more than action; mastering your mistakes more than mastering a moral code.

Key text: The masterpiece associated with the name of Lao Tzu is the *Tao Te Ching*. It is an evocative presentation of the way of life Taoism recommends.

Interesting fact: Lao Tzu means 'Old Master', and so whether the *Tao Te Ching* is the composition of one individual, or the accumulated wisdom of otherwise unknown masters, is up for scholarly dispute.

Varieties of stillness

We'll come to Lao Tzu specifically in a moment, but first consider the nature of stillness, physical and spiritual, for it comes in a variety of forms and promises different things. Think of the stillness of the silences contained in a piece of music, the pregnant rests and dramatic pauses, and the wonderful moment when the piece ends and there's a stillness before the applause begins. It's a kind of stillness that we are in danger of losing.

I remember going to hear a performance of Mahler's Second Symphony, the 'Resurrection', in the enormous space of Westminster Cathedral in London. It is a monumental piece with great drama but also, I learned, deliberate silence. In particular, Mahler left instructions that after the first long movement, an extended meditation on death, there should be a five-minute silence. He felt an audience would gain from a long pause after the turbulent emotions of the movement. In the stillness, the true impact of the music would be felt. This instruction is usually ignored, though for this one performance I attended, the conductor thought he would try it out. He explained to us what would happen.

It didn't work. I recall the person sat next to me opening her handbag and unwrapping a sweet. Someone sat on the other side of her produced the evening paper from her bag, and started to thumb the pages. Only for a few short seconds, amidst the long five minutes, did the audience achieve a momentary stillness. Mostly, the attempted silence was filled with rustling and distractions. It seemed that, even for an audience used to listening to music, stillness was too difficult to do. It reminded me of Blaise Pascal's reflection on the matter: 'All of humanity's problems stem from man's inability to sit quietly in a room alone.'

The stilled mind

A different kind of stillness can come about after a lot of frenetic thought. The philosopher Thomas Aquinas knew this kind of intellectual stillness right at the end of his life. The story goes that on the morning of 6 December 1273 he said mass, as usual. He would normally then have gathered his thoughts, turned to his secretary, and continued with the extraordinary production of words and arguments that was his life's work. His discourse would have continued over the philosophy of nature, logic, metaphysics, morality, mind and theology – a seemingly perpetual motion of thought, emerging from a brilliant and restless mind. Except on that morning, he stopped. He turned to his secretary, and told him: no more. From now on, stillness.

What I think had happened is that Aquinas had reached a point that is to be found only on the other side of the struggle to understand. The philosopher had chosen the greatest struggle of all, the attempt to understand God. But now, after many attempts at that goal, he had appreciated a profound truth. The divine voice is small and still. It's an insight that can only truly be grasped when human agitation has exhausted itself. It's a kind of letting go, and Aquinas let go of his work, though paradoxically he could only experience the stillness having previously given himself whole heartedly to writing all those words. The stillness spoke to him of the mystery of God, which lies beyond human telling. Stillness was the culmination of his search.

> 'Under all speech that is good for anything there lies a silence that is better. Silence is deep as Eternity; speech is shallow as time.'
> Thomas Carlyle

Desert stillness

A different kind of stillness again is in the silence of the hermit. The British writer Sara Maitland explores it in A Book of Silence (2008). She has spent many years in pursuit of silence, but not just any silence – the silence of a country house or the silence of reading – but the kind of silence that instils stillness. She comes to realize that there is no literal silence in life, for there are always gurglings or murmurings or hummings or clunks as part of the background noise, even when she finds herself alone on a Scottish moor. So what makes for the silence she seeks is not so much noise as stillness. She writes: 'there is an interior dimension to silence, a sort of stillness of heart and mind which is not a void but a rich space.'

It's a stillness that can cause panic. There are accounts of explorers travelling to the white stillness of the Antarctic and becoming oppressed by a land in which no birds sing, no water flows, no stones become loose underfoot, no trees catch the wind. 'This stillness,' wrote Goutran de Procius, 'which has been so solitary, which has calmed me and done good to my worn-out nerves, gradually began to weigh on me like a lead weight. The flame of life within us withdrew further and further into a secret hiding place, and our heartbeats became even slower.' He worries the place might kill him with a stillness that paralyses life.

What keeps stillness attractive for Maitland is a different kind of emptying of the self, one that is positive. It's closely associated with the silence of the desert, traditionally the place where religious hermits choose to go. Desert silence, she concludes, precipitates a kenotic response, an emptying of the self that simultaneously opens it up; a sense of transparency and dissolving before the infinity of sand, sun and air. This was what the hermits sought, in their struggle to gain a purity of heart and mind that was open to God.

Silent meditation

Stillness does extraordinary things. It forces you into the present, and thereby into a sense of presence, which must be why Eastern meditation sets such store by it. You can gain a sense of this without the meditation by attending closely to sculptures of the human form, or perhaps an icon of a saint's head gazing out at you. If they're real masterpieces, they will freeze a moment and time. To stare at one is to be exposed to an extraordinary intensity. The intimacy you apparently share with the still figure seems to break into something transcendent. It's not that you half expect them to move, though you do, so much as you half hope they *do* move, in order to break the spell. There's something about the stillness of these figures and images that causes you to reflect upon yourself. The illusion of being watched is, of course, an illusion. But by observing that which is still, a stillness is stirred up in you. In that moment, you may capture a sense of yourself almost free of everyday concerns.

According to Lao Tzu, what stillness releases is a clearer perception of things. It is not an absolute stillness, of course: even the figurative statues and painted icons are not really still, but slowly disintegrating into dust. But it is a relative stillness that allows the flux of life to become more apparent.

In Asian thought, it's called the Tao, the Way. Stillness is recommended as a practice in order to recognize your own participation in that flow, and to become more attune to it. The idea is to put to one side your

Figure 23 Confucius, 551–479 BC, presenting the young Shakyamuni Buddha to Lao Tzu, founder of Chinese Taoism, Wang Shu-Ku painting, 18th century.

own distracting activity and, through non-activity, perceive that everything is in a state of motion. That comes as something of a relief, and generates a sense of peace, because you realize imposing your own activity on the world is more likely than not to be against the Tao, thereby fighting it. The good life is different; to go with the flow, the Way. The Western religious equivalent is the notion of 'letting the spirit flow' or 'resting in God's hands'. The individual still participates in life, but less wilfully, more immediately.

Perfected crafts

It sounds mystical, though many of the examples the Taoist draw on are everyday. Craftsmen are favourite characters. They have perfected their craft by stilling their minds: they do not think about what they are doing, but simply do it. Moreover, if they think about doing it, the perfection they had attained fails them. Lao Tzu describes a draughtsman who can draw a freehand circle, or a right angle, with greater precision than he can with a compass or set square. Or there's the butcher who can carve up an ox with such attunement to the carcass that his knife hasn't had to be sharpened in decades.

It's something akin to what the musician realizes when mastering a piece of music: it's not so much that they are playing the piece, as the music is playing them. The same experience explains why it is easy to play the piece from memory: it is not so much that it is has been memorized, as that the notes can no longer go in any other place. There is a personal stillness, and transparency, that allows something else to come through the individual.

Writing about this kind of experience provokes a number of apparent paradoxes. Lao Tzu revels in them:

'A man of the highest virtue does not keep to virtue and that is why he has virtue. A man of the lowest virtue never strays from virtue and that is why he is without virtue. The former never acts yet leaves nothing undone. The latter acts but there are things left undone.'

The virtue of stillness

Socrates is remembered for a way of life that is similar to Lao Tzu's, and there are some striking accounts of him remaining still, often for some time. One of the most memorable comes in Plato's dialogue, the *Symposium*. One of Socrates' associates, Alcibiades, tells the story:

'One morning he was thinking about something which he could not resolve; he would not give it up, but continued thinking from early dawn until noon – there he stood fixed in thought; and at noon attention was drawn to him, and the rumour ran through the wondering crowd that Socrates had been standing and thinking about something ever since the break of day. At last, in the evening after supper, some Ionians out of curiosity (I should explain that this was not in winter but in summer) brought out their mats and slept in the open air that they might watch him and see whether he would stand all night. There he stood until the following morning; and with the return of light he offered up a prayer to the sun, and went his way.'

The Ionians, and others, took the stillness to be a spectacle. But there is surely a link between his standing still and a Taoist conception of stillness. It is symptomatic of a perception of reality gained by a master.

The ramifications of this become clear in the Socratic idea that true knowledge is the same as true virtue. It clearly doesn't follow that someone who can write and talk about goodness, say, will necessarily be good – any more than the person who can write and talk about music will be a good musician. But that's to interpret knowledge as being an *analysis* of the matter in hand. However, equating virtue with knowledge as an *experience* of the matter in hand transforms the insight. To perceive goodness in this sense is to have known it as manifest in your own life. To that extent, you know what it is to be good. The saint, or sage, would be the individual who knows goodness not just on occasion but continually. It seems that it takes a practice of stillness to achieve it.

There's a wonderful film, *Into Great Silence* (2005) by Philip Gröning, that offers a cinematic taste of stillness. It sounds a struggle: 160 minutes of patchwork scenes from inside the Grande Chartreuse, home of ascetic Carthusian French monks who live silent lives. That there is virtually no talk, and only the intermittent sound of a bell or chant, does not sound encouraging. But the film is beautiful and engrossing. It is a veritable invitation to stillness, on your sofa.

25

Stories – and your moral imagination

THERE *is a tale told by Innana, an Egyptian scribe, which is preserved on a papyrus in the British Museum. It's 3,200 years old, and so is said to be the oldest written story in the world. It concerns two brothers, Anpu and Bata, and what happens when one day Anpu's wife attempts to seduce Bata, her brother-in-law. Honour is, of course, offended. Various escapes and deaths are the result. It tells of how Bata eventually has his revenge. But here's the thing: it is surely no coincidence that this ancient narrative, the oldest, is a moral tale.*

Exemplary stories have always been integral to our attempts to make sense of life and to find a propitious path through it. Today – with our fear of appearing moralistic, with our sensitivity to values different from our own – stories are perhaps the dominant way we address ethical questions. Think of soap operas, reality television, chat shows. . . They are all in the business of telling tales, coloured by ethical imperatives. The kiss-and-tell genre is arguably so popular because we are otherwise so nervous of talking about the good life itself.

What's of value in the best morality tales is not the moral of the tale, though. Some, it's true, have an ethical punchline. Little Red Riding Hood warns kids against strangers. But the best show their insights within the story itself. They don't tell it too explicitly. As Ernest Hemingway put it, 'If I had a message,

I'd send a telegram.' What he's highlighting is that it's the experience of the fiction itself that is so valuable. Therein lies its truth and wisdom. Stories explore what's possible in life. By exercising our imaginative sympathies they engage our moral imagination. The best enlarge our humanity not by addressing us but by drawing out our humanity.

> 'A beginning, a muddle, and an end.'
> Philip Larkin

Leo Tolstoy (1828–1910)

Quick summary: The great Russian novelist and aristocrat often struggled with life, not least his wealthy inheritance. He found satisfaction in a humble asceticism that in turn inspired others as far away as India and America to a 'Tolstoyan' way of life.

Key text: His big novels are *Anna Karenina* (1873–7), his exploration of passionate love, and *War and Peace* (1865–7), his exploration of violent conflict. His philosophy of life is conveyed in *A Confession* (1882).

Interesting fact: As a child, his brother had told him a story about a hidden key that unlocked a door to a Golden Age. As an old man, Tolstoy asked to be buried in the secret spot his brother had revealed to him.

* * * * * * * * * * * * * * * * * * *

Figure 24 Tolstoy portrayed as 'The Man of Truth'.

Windows on to souls

Stories are so morally valuable because they enable us to experience life vicariously – as if we are inhabiting someone else's life. In this way, they can massively widen our experience of life. Stories provide us with a window into other people's souls, a microscope with which to study the inner workings of another's consciousness, though without being so intrusive. Tolstoy is a master narrator in this sense. Consider his short story 'Happy Ever After', also known as 'Family Happiness' (this can be found in *The Death of Ivan Ilych and Other Stories* (Penguin Classics) translated by Rosemary Edmonds).

It is the story of an unremarkable marriage. A middle-aged man, Sergey, meets a younger woman, Masha. They fall in love, marry, run into a rough patch in their marriage, and find a way through it.

Now, summarized that way, the message of the story seems plain and obvious. The moral is that love has its seasons. Unless a relationship can change, so as to flourish in the dog days of its summer, as well as the springtime of its youth, then it will not be a love that lasts.

But such verities, which are blindingly obvious to most, are also more or less useless as guides to life. What's missing is the experience Sergey and Masha undergo. Catch a glimpse of that, and the story becomes a vehicle of wisdom. That is what Tolstoy provides so copiously.

Narrative truth

Tolstoy tells his tale through the person of Masha. She conveys her inner experience, and so allows the reader to live it too. So, as Masha is leaving her youthful hopes behind, and becoming disillusioned with their marriage, she muses:

'All that I had hardly dared to hope for had come to pass. My vague confused dreams had become a reality, and the reality had become an oppressive, difficult, and joyless life. All remained the same – the garden visible through the window, the grass, the path, the very same bench, the same song of the nightingale by the pond, the same lilacs in full bloom, the same moon shining above the house; and yet, in everything such a terrible inconceivable change! Such coldness in all that might have been near and dear!'

We can feel it, as we can Masha's growing guilt at having such thoughts. She worries that if their love has died, then perhaps she is responsible. They talk. (It's the one thing they never fail to get right.) And in that talking she finds redemption. In fact, their talking is itself a kind of retelling of their story that they relate to themselves. For as they talk she is able to identify a different narrative for their ongoing life together. Reflecting on her experience brings a new awareness in Masha. She continues:

'I looked at him, and suddenly my heart grew light; it seemed that the cause of my suffering had been removed like an aching nerve. Suddenly I realized clearly and calmly that the past feeling, like the past time itself, was gone beyond recall, and that it would be not only impossible but painful and uncomfortable to bring it back. And after all, was that time so good which seemed to me so happy?'

She realizes that what has happened to them is inevitable, even benign. Young love has to die to make way for something else, and with that insight, born of reconceiving her life, she is released from the tyranny of her longings. Sergey explains that everyone 'must have personal experience of all the nonsense of life, in order to get back to life itself; the evidence of other people is no good.' Again, that parallels the experience Tolstoy's novel itself offers.

With a different narrative in place, a different kind of happiness becomes possible for Masha, a new foundation for life: such is the power of the new story she is able to relate to herself about herself. Such is the power of Tolstoy's story for his readers – who will probably have experienced the power of love and puzzled over its transformations too – that they might be in a position to discover a new path that their own life may take, to find a new story for themselves, only now written by themselves.

> 'The central function of imaginative literature
> is to make you realize that other people act on
> moral convictions different from your own.'
> William Empson

Truth games

Stories might be thought of as games that people can play with the narratives of their lives. And like the games children play, they are very serious. Remember playing hide-and-seek? The thrill of the game is in being lost and then found, more excitement being derived the longer you are left unfound – so long as you are found *eventually*. In other words, it is a game that allows a child to come to terms with the isolation it experiences when alone. Play the game well, and you may be able to cope better with feeling isolated as a grown-up, later in life.

What narrative games also make possible is toying with forces and feelings that you don't wholly understand and can't completely control. They are, therefore, unlike work. If you work on something, you proceed on the basis that there is a task to be completed. It can be clearly described, carefully managed, diligently pursued and is amenable to having goals and outcomes assessed. But although we sometimes say that we are *working* on this or that aspect of our lives, we might do better to *play* at it a little – in all seriousness. To experiment with a few alternative tellings. For then we can bring into play the forces and feelings that a more linear approach would push to one side.

Stories are 'life gaming'. They allow you to entertain uncertain possibilities. They offer you scenarios that are not possible to pursue in life. Witness the popularity of crime and thrillers. By imaginatively entering the terrain of murder and fear, you gain insight into options that if you actually chose them in life would lead to calamity and real danger.

There is a truth to be discovered in this process. For all that fictions are just that, fictions, their lack of literal, empirical truth frees them from what Oscar Wilde called 'the monstrous worship of facts'. That freedom is of immense worth. It creates the creative space to make the move from what is the case in your life, through what *ought to be* the case, to what can *become* the case.

Character, not closure

It follows that the good life is hugely dependent upon the quality of the stories around, at any given time. A society that is rich in myths and narratives will be one in which human flourishing is possible. A society that censors its narratives will be not only a cultural desert but a dry land for human life too. Diversity is key: our moral imaginations flourish best in a narrative Amazon.

Moreover, there will be no end to the telling of stories, and if there were – if the tales stopped – our humanity would start to contract. Narrative is therefore a kind of negative activity, an unsaying of what has been said, and a commitment to continuation, refusing closure. The aim is not to find an ultimate narrative that once told stops all other retellings, but just to keep telling. Similarly, the virtues and characters that moral tales nurture can never be conclusively defined, as they must be constantly remade in real lives. The moral life, so conceived, is not a rational quest to find the right rules and regulations, but is a courageous quest to keep the story of life going.

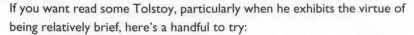
A Step

If you want read some Tolstoy, particularly when he exhibits the virtue of being relatively brief, here's a handful to try:

- 'Happy Ever After', to experience how to fall in love and survive the disillusion.
- 'The Cossacks', to experience disenchantment tended by the beauty of nature in the wild.
- 'My Confession', to experience how to have a crisis of faith and recover.
- 'The Death of Ivan Ilyich', to experience how to live badly but die well.

26

Tolerance – or the wisdom of others

WE live in a world of truths, of multiple values and virtues. It's not that there is no truth in the twenty-first century, as postmodernists have said. It's rather that different people hold to different values and certainties with, apparently, equally strong conviction. Optimists affirm humankind's essential goodness; Christians humankind's 'fallen' nature; and Buddhists say that we won't get anywhere until we recognize life's essential quality of suffering.

The good, the bad and the ugly. These different truths are neither easily compared, because they presume different world views, nor is it obvious how they can all be true. 'We can reason,' affirms the optimist, 'and that is why there is ground for hope.' 'Oh no,' declares the Christian, 'God's truth is folly to human minds.' 'But you both miss the point,' continues the Buddhist, 'you're clinging to your faith in reason or God, when in truth, that clinging is the cause of the suffering.'

So how can we live in this world of multiplicity? It's tough, not just because we might be divided from others. But because we might also be divided within ourselves, that inner conflict which like a civil war risks the worst acts of violence. What virtue is required? Tolerance.

Modernity's car crash

Tolerance appears to be an art form that is disappearing in the modern world. A growing number of issues – some important, some strikingly small – provoke bitter discontent in the public square. Different places draw up different battle lines. In the United States, one can point to abortion, gay marriage and Darwinian evolution. In the United kingdom, the list would include faith schools, voluntary euthanasia and religious broadcasting. In France, it's different again – religious dress and ethnicity.

Of course, there is a limit to tolerance, beyond which it ceases to be a virtue and becomes a vice of injustice or appeasement or naivety. But that does not seem to be our problem today. Rather, what's striking is that we who live in these countries mostly have vast amounts in common. So how is it that we live in a world that can car-crash over such specific, and apparently insurmountable, differences? And why should we care?

> *'Human diversity makes tolerance more than a virtue, it makes it a requirement for survival.'*
> René Dubos

Desiderius Erasmus (1466–1536)

Quick summary: A priest and philosopher, Erasmus came from lowly means and ended up perhaps the greatest scholar of his generation.

Key text: *In Praise of Folly*, written in a week in 1509.

Interesting fact: When correcting the Vulgate version of the New Testament, he phrased the first sentence of John's gospel as 'In the beginning was the Conversation' – not 'the word'.

Brave humour

Erasmus lived through a turbulent period of history, the Reformation. His good friend Thomas More – whom Erasmus memorably called 'a man for all seasons' – was just one notable individual who lost his head. When More was executed, Erasmus celebrated his friend as a genius 'such that England never had and never again will have its like'. His liberality was brave.

And for sure, Erasmus himself was not infrequently in danger. He was later accused of having 'laid the egg that hatched the Reformation', and the wars of religion that followed were some of the bloodiest in European history, as religious arguments became entangled with national interests. It was a heady moment, and yet Erasmus maintained his good humour – another important quality tolerance requires.

But it was the kind of humour that has bite too. When More wrote his famous book, *Utopia*, it was a response to Erasmus's *In Praise of Folly*. Erasmus had written, 'No state has been so plagued by its rulers as when power has fallen into the hands of some dabbler in philosophy.' *Utopia*, a word More coined, means 'no place' – wittily implying a similar point: philosopher-kings should think but may be rulers of no place. Hence Socrates had been a gadfly, nipping the back of the noble and proud thoroughbred that was ancient Athens. Erasmus would do the same. Tolerance can have bite.

Figure 25 Desiderius *Erasmus* (1523) by Hans Holbein the Younger (1497/9–1543), Germany.

The truth will out

The nature of Erasmus's capacity for tolerance comes across in other ways too. He advocated religious toleration, and for an interesting reason. People hold their strongest convictions for all kinds of ambiguous and unclear reasons, he thought. Dissent is, therefore, a virtue as it brings shadowy motivations to light, and makes subtle reasoning clearer. The truth will out, it is often said – though only if the right spirit is abroad in the minds of individuals like Erasmus.

Such principles became his practice particularly in relation to his relationship with Martin Luther. The two men admired each other because Erasmus concurred that the Church was in need of reform. However, he resisted joining Luther's crusade, and when the Pope condemned the latter, Erasmus attempted to get Luther to moderate his language. The reason was not fear of debate: the two argued fiercely about the nature of free will. It was rather that when reasoned debate turns to violent conflict, truth is always the victim. 'I doubt that either side can be suppressed without grave loss,' he reflected: human beings must converse, as the truth is greater than any one individual can embrace. It's a reflection of intellectual humility, which is also important for nurturing tolerance.

Erasmus died of natural causes, and as a Catholic, though it's striking that his translation of the Bible became the standard among Protestants. Moreover, later on, his books were censored by the Catholic Church, when they were placed on the List of Prohibited Books. Perhaps this suggests another characteristic of tolerance: for all that it is resisted, even loathed, by lesser men, it transcends their conflicts and appeals to a better part in us. Throughout his life, Erasmus argued that healthy diversity is a sign of the search for underlying unity, and that even if that unity remains elusive, tolerance of itself does not undermine the goal. It is fear and panic about the search which achieves that.

'Hear the other side.'
Saint Augustine

The great leveller

So Erasmus sets a standard. But what of our situation today? It's the difficulty of living quite similarly, though with a few marked differences, that goes to the heart of the challenge now. It is often referred to as the *narcissism of small differences* – the foul feeling that emerges between individuals who are really quite like each other. Freud described it this way: 'Intolerance of groups is often, strangely enough, exhibited more strongly against small differences than against fundamental ones.'

This source of intolerance is magnified in the modern world as a by-product of globalization. It undermines our sense of identity by encouraging us to treat ourselves in much the same way, regardless of where we live and what we do. Consumerism as the great leveller. But when everyone wears T-shirts and drinks cola, everyone also feels the loss of something to make them stand out, to preserve a distinctive sense of self.

Some buy an expensive T-shirt and call it their style; or drink a different brand of cola and call it their choice. And such small differences become very important. I'm told that among the gangs of south London your life can depend on the type of trainers you wear. In the gated communities of west London the same ostracizing dynamic is in operation, only the markers there are attached to Chelsea tractors and delis with Italian names.

God wars

But this raises another exacerbating problem. Such markers don't run very deep. A T-shirt is, after all, just two cuts of cotton stitched around the side, whether it comes from Primark or Gucci. Take a different marker though – like some kind of religious commitment, or a conviction about the godlessness of the cosmos – and that can go deeper, perhaps to the core of your being. Such traditions are more profound than mere questions of style. They tell you where you belong and with whom you belong. They help you orient yourself as you traverse an otherwise flattened ideological landscape.

It's no surprise, then, that the twenty-first century has so far been marked by 'God wars'. Again, what's striking about them is that they are conducted by individuals who are otherwise really quite similar – similar classes, education, ethnicity, ethos. . . But for that very reason, the psychological importance of whether you believe the world was created in six days or about four and a half billion years is enormous. There's an academic debate to have about such questions, of course. But emotionally, what matters is to belong to one side or the other.

Everything you hold dear is then staked according to whether you're a Darwinist or a Creationist, whether you keep a Bible on your shelf or a copy of the *Origin of Species*. They represent lines in the sand that you will not cross; markers against which to measure whether your world stands or falls. Intolerance is the way to revel in the difference.

Respect yourself

Respect is another word for tolerance that has been a virtue in the public square, a prerequisite for engaging in debate. The ethic is still rehearsed in the British parliamentary formality of referring to Members of Parliament as 'honourable'. That the practice sounds old-fashioned or eccentric is a sign of the erosion of tolerance. And it seems to be disappearing in a particular way.

Sticking with examples from the God wars: those without religion can fail to show respect for the beliefs of others, with some secularists going so far as to make a virtue of showing disrespect. Why should I recognize your sacred text, they ask? I regard it as so much rubbish. It works the other way round too. Believers can be just as disinclined to respect secular convictions about human rights or freedom of speech. And again, that goes to the extent of dismissing some claims for the very reason that they are demanded by right.

Respect matters in tolerance not because of some nostalgic desire for a lost world in which we doffed hats and were called by our surnames. It matters because if I show you respect it signifies that I'm giving you the time of day. It means I'm treating you as a person. Moreover, it recognizes that I might learn something from you if I do. And I might learn something about myself too – that most difficult category of knowledge.

Erasmus had this kind of respect. It showed in his relationship with Luther and the Pope, two individuals otherwise on different sides of an ideological divide. It takes courage to try to straggle it, and intellectual humility, though remember too his humour and bite. Respect does not mean retreat.

Which is why it was a virtue recognized by the early philosophers of the Enlightenment period too, as crucial for any flourishing public square. And the public square mattered to them a lot. They believed that it is only by debating openly, generously and honestly that human beings can hope to move towards the state called enlightenment. We simply can't do it alone, or in like-minded groups. That way serves merely to reinforce ignorance. If everyone speaks just as they will, and blindly follows the turbulent currents of their own free thought, then the result is not progress but anarchy, and quite probably violence. 'What is objectionable, what is dangerous about extremists,' noted Robert F Kennedy, 'is not that they are extreme but that they are intolerant.'

Tolerance demands that we listen to others, as well as expect to be listened to; we must respect others, for it is only in so doing that we truly respect ourselves. It's been called the *principle of humanity*. It means that you've got to sit down and talk with your opponent.

To put it another way, the Enlightenment clarion call – 'Dare to know!' – implies the corollary of daring to know you might be wrong, and daring to be different. Someone who speaks only to express themselves, who only exercises their free speech, is never going to know any difference. Someone who fails to show respect sets their face against enlightenment. Conversely, the good society is one in which human relations are characterized by goodwill. It's not a call to agree. It's a call to want to understand.

When people take offence, that process is hindered. When they immediately head for the bunkers, or run to the law, our collective humanity is diminished. Enlightenment slips back over the horizon along with the standard for engagement Erasmus defined.

So here's the crucial issue, I think. Tolerance has to do with human diversity flourishing, not out of some notion of political correctness, but out of a recognition that to be human is to be flawed. No one has the complete answer, which is precisely why people disagree. The pluralism of our times is evidence enough that no one world view is satisfactory enough.

We need others because with others we can detect the errors in our own perceptions. Conversely, those who cannot tolerate others are likely to fear their own flaws, their own weaknesses. 'Bigotry tries to keep truth safe in its hand with a grip that kills it,' thought Rabindranath Tagore. What must we do? Release that grip.

27

Uncertainty – and the value of doubt

DOUBT, *and its rich collection of associated fears, are part and parcel of the human condition. Uncertainty is a prime candidate for one of the capacities that distinguishes us from other animals. Does a dung beetle fret about the meaning of its existence? Does a mayfly worry about tomorrow? We do, many of us much of the time.*

The cause of this restlessness is accounted for in a number of ways. Socrates had a good suggestion. He realized that human beings are bemused about many things – where we can find satisfaction; what way to do politics; why there's something we call the universe, and not simply nothing at all. But what's doubly troubling about being bemused is that you know it; you aren't just ignorant, but are fully conscious of your ignorance too.

The Nobel Prize-winning biologist Tim Hunt believes something similar is integral to science. It's like turning over stones, he says, only to find another stone, down and down and down. 'You are never quite sure where you are,' he explains. 'You've got to enjoy swimming in this sea of unknowing, because otherwise what's the point.'

Socrates continued with the observation that the consciousness of not knowing is both a curse and a blessing. It's a blessing in that it powers us to want to understand. It's a curse in that, when we tire of the doubt that surrounds us, we become frustrated, or worse. What's the point? Uncertainty is cousin to despair and ennui. It's an existential complaint.

Which also explains why fundamentalism and fanaticism are ever appealing to human beings. Their false promise is the banishment of uncertainty for ever.

> *'I lived uncertain, I die doubtful: O thou Being of beings, have mercy upon me!'*
>
> Aristotle, attributed last words

Emily Dickinson (1830–86)

Quick summary: Most of the American poet Emily Dickinson's work was not published until after her death. Uncertainty and mortality are two of its abiding themes.

Key text: Her collected poems are now widely available, her genius having been recognized in the late twentieth century.

Interesting fact: Dickinson was a recluse, and later in life even refused to leave her room, though she had many friends, maintained by correspondence.

Dying belief

What makes Emily Dickinson such a wise figure on doubt is that she lived in an age of profound uncertainty. Hers was the generation that witnessed an historic collapse in the consolations of religious faith. Along with other Victorians, she saw the possibility of belief evaporating like morning mist. And yet, she was different from

Figure 26 An early photograph of Emily Dickinson.

other poets who, like Matthew Arnold, wrote of faith's 'long, withdrawing roar', and philosophers who announced the 'death of God'. She resisted that spirit and by exploring the ambiguities of uncertainty, rather than simply yielding to it, found a path in between triumphant belief and troubled doubt. She worked out how to handle the limits of human understanding, and transform uncertainty into a source of human meaning.

Poetry was her medium. It allowed her to express both the desire for assurance and the anxiety that it had disappeared. With it, she could measure the longing and the loss, and in so doing stay with it. And then came an unexpected consequence. For in recognizing doubt for what it is, she found her humanity affirmed. Uncertainty turns out to have an expansive quality, for all that it troubles. There is virtue in the courageous embrace of life, in all its fearful fullness.

Doubt's surprise

My favourite poem in which she expresses something of this has the opening two lines, 'Tell all the Truth but tell it slant – | Success in Circuit lies.' In short, we humans are like crabs: we make progress by walking sideways.

Only it's hard to walk sideways when your eyes are in the front of your head. You bump into things. And further, our binocular vision creates a delusion. We presume that the truth is in front of us too. What we forget is that, not knowing the truth, the chances of us looking in the direction in which it is to be found are slight. Instead, if we're lucky, we glimpse it in our peripheral vision, out of the corner of one eye. This is truth's 'superb surprise'. We should not be offended by the fact that the truth is too bright 'for our infirm Delight'. The poem concludes: 'The Truth must dazzle gradually | Or every man be blind –'.

Prayer's expression

The theme of truth's concealment is close to another secret: the hiddenness of God. This was something that all mystics have explored, though Dickinson approaches it with a twist. For Saint Paul, the truth is seen through a glass darkly, and the divine is celebrated at an altar to the unknown God. But that God exists was not itself doubted by the great missionary. Dickinson, though, lived in the age that took the extra step. If God is unknown, maybe that's because God is not.

The pain of that possibility comes out in her poems on prayer. For her, to pray is the supreme expression of the uncertain soul. It is an activity that confirms an absence, not reveals a presence. She acknowledges that praying might be a kind of wish fulfilment, as the Victorian psychoanalysts would conclude. And she's also quite aware that prayer might be the tragic habit of the human creature who would otherwise be crushed by the weight of cosmic meaninglessness. 'They fling their Speech,' she writes, 'By means of it – in God's ear.' And they keep flinging, though any hearing is denied. Dickinson, for one, has to acknowledge that she cannot expect any answers.

This is a moment of profound risk, one that mirrors the moment when an individual becomes so panicked by uncertainty that they flip and become a fundamentalist or fanatic. For doubt's disappointment can turn to bitterness when a prayer is spurned. The individual who is unskilled in uncertainty is like the child who, after their first experience of being duped by an adult, locks themselves in their room in order to be alone. The care they'd relied on is apparently snatched from them and, with its removal, the seeds of distrust are sown. They learn a suspicion of the world, a frame of mind that throws away love and expectancy and delight.

If suspicion doubts whether the cosmos cares, it next provokes a sense that life itself does not care, and then the further feeling that, maybe, we should not care for life. Would it not have been more loving of God, or nature, to have left us 'in the Atom's Tomb – | Merry, and Nought, and gay, and numb – | Than this smart Misery', Dickinson asks. Conned, like kids who grow up disillusioned, we are left with a gnawing sense of emptiness, and are tempted to lash out. Understanding is misery. Ignorance is no longer bliss.

> *'The trouble with the world is that the stupid*
> *are cocksure and the intelligent are full of*
> *doubt.'*
>
> Bertrand Russell

Ignorance and awe

However, there is another facet of doubt that can be recovered and become compelling. It's not so much about hope, as awe. In another poem, Dickinson likens her search to knocking on the door of a house that is apparently unoccupied, of hoping for the warmth of its hearth and fire when there is no sign of smoke rising from the chimney. Instead, one is confronted with 'Vast Prairies of Air'. Her traveller is mocked by the lack of a reply, and left thinking, 'Infinitude – Had'st Thou no Face | That I might look on Thee?' And yet, with that sense of infinitude comes something else: a sense of wonder.

Dickinson is back to that most profound of questions: Why is there something rather than nothing? And ignorance is itself what generates the sense of awe she feels. That she can just ask the question is, in fact, enough. Here, then, is the key to handling our unknowingness. It's why asking better questions can be genuinely more satisfying than reaching final answers. It's why turning over stone after stone after stone can become a fascinating way of life.

It's rather like the reflection of another poet, Samuel Taylor Coleridge. In *Aids to Reflection* (1825), he wrote: 'In Wonder all Philosophy began; in Wonder it ends: and Admiration fill up the interspace. But the first Wonder is the offspring of Ignorance: the last is the parent of Adoration.' The consciousness of not knowing leads to wonderment, so long as the individual has the capacity to remain with the doubt. This capacity is what another poet again, John Keats, called 'negative capability': 'that is when man is capable of being in uncertainties, mysteries, doubts, without any irritable reaching after fact and reason.'

To put it another way, you do not have to know the answer for a great question to remind you of the heights and depths to which the human imagination can aspire. Uncertainty should not be abandoned, for the sake of the human spirit. This helps explain why it is those who have no doubts who seem less than human to us, not those who have them. They are frightening, monstrous, because they don't doubt they are right.

The negative way

Dickinson comes to be sure of one thing: without this mystery, humanity shrivels; or as she writes: 'The abdication of Belief | Makes the Behavior small.' She's unlike the atheists of her time, in sensing that the erosion of Christianity does not lead to the exaltation of humanity, as if the two elements were on opposite sides of a seesaw, so that one rises up only because the other dips down. Rather, she sees that humanity and spirituality are one of a kind: let doubt disenchant the world, by ignoring the vitality of life and instead extolling its mechanistic nature, and human beings inevitably come to look like little more than well-engineered machines.

But the wheels of the seasons, and the cogs of life, do not aimlessly turn. Poetry itself is premised on as much. For Dickinson, the very possibility of poetry rests on the truth that humanity, and by extension nature, are not merely the product of blind processes. At the very least, as Walt Whitman put it, we can, like fledged birds, 'rise and fly and sing' for ourselves.

Dickinson herself resorts to the analogy of a house, again. (By the time she wrote this poem, she had confined herself to her own house.) She observes that a house requires scaffolding to be built. And once built, and the props are removed, the well-built house will be able to stand of its accord. Is that the stage of development we've reached in the age of doubt? Is it one in which the old props can be removed and, though feeling the full force of uncertainty, we can still stand?

The practice of doubt

To be honest, Dickinson is not sure whether her analogy itself stands. If the human spirit is capable of great things, it's also deeply flawed. Fundamentalism and fanaticism are equally likely outcomes. She reflects on ladders; they allow you to ascend higher, though with the corollary that you have further to fall should fear grip you and you look down.

However, the negative way of doubt is, in fact, essential to being open to newness. That follows because we can only fully say 'yes' to what we already know and grasp. So a negative dialectic, paradoxically, has the capacity to lead us to new worlds, towards that which is beyond our comprehension, to the transcendent.

Similarly, if human beings abandon their imagination and turn their backs on the quest that their questioning makes possible, then the culture that follows is depleted. This is the outcome of failing to live well with uncertainty. We give up on the greatest good, and opt instead for the good enough. We abandon the quest for truth, and stay with answers determined by what works. We lose touch with that which might be of great worth, even though it remains unclear, for fear that it mocks our ignorance like the distant proof to an unsolved mathematical puzzle. But the human world, and with it the human spirit, gradually, relentlessly, grows smaller.

Keep swimming in the sea of unknowing, Dickinson is saying – or better, write poetry. Though if, like me, you doubt you can do that, then at least read it. For poetry is often the best medium for exploring uncertainty, by virtue of the fact that it can glimpse what lies in our peripheral vision, that it can see *sideways*. It keeps expansiveness a possibility. It offers truth's superb surprise.

28

Wisdom – also called 'love's knowledge'

WE *moderns absorb facts and figures as readily as we breathe the clean air. We trust them. They are our benchmark for truth. So it may appear mistaken to suggest that wisdom could be closer to compassion than pure knowledge.*

Pascal, whose grasp of mathematics provided the groundwork for one of the sciences of figures – probability – was alive to the alternative link. There is a connection, say, between knowing someone and loving them: it is not true, as is often said, that you must understand someone before you can properly love them, but rather it's the case that you get to know someone only because you loved them first. You must first long for what you seek if you are to find it. The scientist in her lab, engaged in decades of research with no guarantee of progress, appreciates this as keenly as the artist in his studio.

Moreover, it's compassion when coupled to understanding that yields wisdom, not understanding alone. Compassion does not just ask about the *truth* of things but seeks the *worth* of things. It assesses what might be esteemed as of greater or lesser value. Which all implies that the philosopher, the lover of wisdom, must nurture their capacity to love as much as their capacity to think. As the Buddhist metaphor has it, the bird must have both wings in order to take flight.

The French essayist Michel de Montaigne noticed something similar. It struck him that the good life is often portrayed as a great struggle between conflicting desires, or as an heroic ability to face agony and pain stoically. But then he noticed a richer way of life, one different from that borne by such 'stiff souls'. It was the way of life lived by compassionate souls, individuals with a deep sensitivity to the world around them. This struck him as truly wise because it enlarges our humanity. He concluded that the greatest barrier to wisdom is not ignorance but cruelty.

> 'To see it without feeling it is not to know it.'
> Jean-Jacques Rousseau

Martha Nussbaum (b. 1947)

Quick summary: Nussbaum has written extensively on moral philosophy, not least about what she calls 'the fragility of goodness', the notion that what good human beings seek is vulnerable to all kinds of threat.

Key text: *The Fragility of Goodness* (1986) is her exploration of moral ideas in Plato and Aristotle and ancient Greek tragedy. Her examination of love and wisdom is found in a fascinating paper, 'Love's Knowledge'.

Interesting fact: With another philosopher, Amartya Sen, Nussbaum also works on the 'capability approach' to assessing quality of life. It does not use Gross National Product as a means of assessing national development, but the extent to which a society allows individuals to flourish in basic 'capabilities', to work, play, organize, love.

A wise heart

We can call it *love's knowledge*. It's the insight someone gains because their compassion has been stirred, often as a result of a painful experience. The pain breaks through the protective barriers of reason to reveal insights that reason alone can't contain.

Nussbaum finds a classic account of such an experience in Marcel Proust's novel *In Search of Lost Time* (translated by C.K. Moncrieff) (Vintage Classics, 1996). There is a moment in the story when Marcel, the main character, realizes that he loves the woman Albertine. But here's the twist: he only knows that he loves her when she has left him. He hadn't been troubled by the prospect of being without her up to that point. He thought he knew he was indifferent to her. And yet, when his heart, as opposed to his head, is stirred by her leaving, an entirely different perception of the situation overwhelms him. He can think of little else but her. Proust provides a record of Marcel's thoughts:

'My imagination sought her in the skies, on evenings like those when we were still able to gaze at it together; I tried to wing my affections towards her, beyond the moonlight that she loved, to console her for no longer being alive, and this love for a person who had become so remote was like a religion, my thoughts rose toward her like prayers.'

Figure 27 Wisdom and compassion have long been linked in Eastern thought, as in this Chinese bodhisattva of Infinite Compassion and Mercy.

It's a familiar experience. Parting makes the heart grow fonder, it is said. Only Proust pushes his examination of the truism a stage further, and this reveals something else about love's knowledge. When Marcel starts to tell his friends and acquaintances about his loss, he simultaneously realizes that his sadness at losing her is already lessening. His heart is telling his head something else he didn't know. Again, it's one step ahead of his rational self, and he has to learn to listen.

For example, one evening the duchesse de Guermantes invites him to the opera.

'But I replied sadly: "No, I cannot go to the theatre, I have lost a friend. She was very dear to me." The tears nearly came to my eyes as I said it and yet for the first time I felt something akin to pleasure in talking about it. It was from that moment that I started to write to everyone to tell them of my great sorrow and to cease to feel it.'

So how is it that Marcel's heart is ahead of him, that it informs him about what he's experiencing much more accurately than his attempts to understand? Love's knowledge, or wisdom, arises from the interplay of the emotional and the rational going on inside us. The mind tries to understand what's going on, but it can do so only by rationalizing the situation, as Marcel does when writing to decline the invitation of the duchesse by saying he has lost a dear friend. But even as he writes, he perceives this is not quite right. And this makes way for another facility to step in, the compassionate facility of the heart.

It yields an understanding of the situation that is better, something the mind alone could not find. Marcel is not actually so sad. He is already getting over Albertine. That comes as a revelation. The heart is an educator, and as a result we are a little wiser. 'Knowledge of the heart must come from the heart,' Nussbaum explains, 'from and in its pains and longings, its emotional responses.'

Refining feeling

Love's knowledge might also be called a training and refinement of feeling, and it was something the novelist E. M. Forster was interested in too. Many of his characters gain a true understanding of what the good life consists in only when they have discarded what they thought they knew about it. Typically it is love that explodes their delusions and, though the experience is painful, their compassion is stirred and they become much wiser about life as a result.

In *A Room with a View* (1908), E.M. Forster describes how Lucy Honeychurch awakens to love's knowledge when she realizes she is in love with George. For most of the novel, she won't allow herself to acknowledge the fact because she thinks she knows her own mind on the matter: she does not love George, but Cecil. She is refusing to hear the wisdom of her heart.

In this uneducated state, the future looks bleak for Lucy. Forster describes how such individuals become cynical, hypocritical and uncomfortable with life. But Lucy is lucky, though she does not think so at the time. Love's knowledge bursts upon her because, like Marcel, she comes to her wit's end. Her breakdown is precipitated by Mr Emerson, George's father, who tells her that she will never know beauty and passion unless she acknowledges that she loves George. In an instant, Lucy sees it and, luckily for her, her heart doesn't allow her to ignore it.

Again, Lucy has first to admit that she knows less about herself, and the world around her, than she thought she did. Only then can love's wisdom begin to dawn on her. She was very certain that she loved Cecil, her assertions of certainty growing more pronounced as a barrier against the truth of the situation. If Proust shows us that love's knowledge is brought about by the pain of compassion, Forster adds that it is brought about by the pain of uncertainty too. When the mind does not know, love's voice can speak.

A spiritual being has 'the weight of the will and of love, wherein appears the worth of everything to be sought, or to be avoided.'

Saint Augustine

Compassion and size

These two literary scenarios focus on what might be called the romantic experience of love's knowledge. But it extends into other spheres of life too. For example, compassion has the ability intuitively to assess what Nussbaum calls the 'size' of what's at stake, how weighty it is. The mind alone finds it hard to grasp the significance of death, say, because death is so hard rationally to grasp. Which is why people say that they understood how painful it is to lose a loved one only when they lost someone themselves.

Such a death will automatically stir the heart, perhaps violently. The individual will not, then, be able to ignore it, but although the emotion may periodically be overwhelming, there will also be moments when they are able to grasp something of what has happened. Mourning might be defined as gradually understanding love's knowledge of the loss. It is not that the pain goes away. Love does not offer closure. What it does offer, though, is insight into what's happened, particularly in relation to the weight of the loss, the preciousness of the love. With time, this allows the individual to live with the loss, and grow wiser about the love they have known.

An example of that wisdom is provided by Montaigne, when he reflected on what he knew in his relationship with his soulmate, Etienne de La Boëtie. What love's knowledge revealed to him, which he conveys in his essay 'On Friendship', has become one of the most moving, and wise, analyses of friendship in Western philosophy.

'In everything we were halves: I feel I am stealing his share from him. Nor is it right for me to enjoy pleasures, I decided, while he who shared things with me is absent from me. I was already used and accustomed to being, in everything, one of two, that I now feel I am no more than a half. There is no deed nor thought in which I do not miss him.'

It's an essay full of pain and insight, the two intimately linked like compassion and wisdom. Montaigne was able to capture a truth about close friendship, that they were 'one soul in two bodies', something he never fully appreciated when Etienne was alive. That's love's knowledge. It tells him that the death is one of the most sizable and serious events of his life.

Compassion and wonder

Montaigne's experience explains another truism about love, that we often don't realize what we have until it is lost. It is hard for us to admit how vulnerable we are, how fragile the good things of life can be, until love's knowledge reveals their precariousness and preciousness. The wisdom we gain is not just valuable for the light it casts on our predicament. As it is based upon compassion, it can be redirected towards others, and shown as sympathy. It's perhaps why many religious traditions not only have stories about compassionate deities, but deities whose compassion is itself born of suffering. Zeus grieved for his son. Jesus suffers on the cross. A bodhisattva has found release from the distress of life but returns as now best placed to help those still trapped by its delusions.

And there is a further dimension to love's knowledge, which is key to expanding our humanity too. It sparks wonder at life itself. To reach out to another, in sympathy, and so treat them as worthy of concern, is to recognize their humanity. It's an instance of what Iris Murdoch referred to as love being the painful realization that others exist. Nussbaum takes it further, extending the compassion and wonder to all sentient creatures:

'When I see with compassion the beating of an animal, a wonder at the complex living thing itself is likely to be mixed with my compassion, and to support it. (Thus we rarely have compassion for the deaths of creatures, such as mosquitos and slugs, toward whom we do not have wonder.)'

Love's knowledge works to extend the boundaries of what we know to be meaningful in the world. The fruit of wisdom is wonder, as the fruit of understanding is compassion.

A Step

Love's knowledge is experienced most powerful as a result of an upheaval in life. However, it can be known in more modest ways too, simply by experimenting with small gestures of compassion towards others. Try offering some cash to the wayfarer on the street, and see what it tells you about yourself and them. And there's a kind of revelatory concern that can be extended to objects too. Instead of discarding a cracked mug, or holed pair of gloves, try mending them. Caring for your stuff might change your experience of the world too.

29

Wonder – in the ordinary

WONDER is a vitally important virtue for us humans. It's largely a question of cultivation. The trick is to see the wonder that lies underneath and through the everyday. It was a skill, a sixth sense, that William James spotted and studied. He has some ideas about its awakening and development.

William James (1842–1910)

Quick summary: A philosopher too, of the pragmatist school, James was one of the founding fathers of psychology, particularly the psychology of religion, and never lost sight of the fact that human experience always exceeds science's ability to categorize and contain it.

Key text: *The Varieties of Religious Experience* (1902) examines what it says on the cover, and his essays are stimulating reads too, not least 'On a Certain Blindness in Human Beings', which provides the ideas for this chapter.

Interesting fact: He was brother of the novelist Henry James and godson to Ralph Waldo Emerson.

. . . .

> *'The larger the shoreline of knowledge, the longer the shoreline of wonder.'*
> American proverb

The excitement of reality

James understood that wonder is closely associated with worth. 'Wherever a process of life communicates an eagerness to him who lives it, there the life becomes genuinely significant,' he wrote. That eagerness can be found in a myriad of ways. For some, it comes with physical activity – the rhythm of running, the exhilaration of the chase; for others it's senses and sights. Others again find their wonder triggered by the imagination, that which takes them beyond the confines of their own experiences and allows them to enter into the lives of others. And then there's the astonishment of contemplation, whether of a mathematical equation or of the deity. 'But, wherever it is found,' James continues, 'there is the zest, the tingle, the excitement of reality.'

How is it that the reality which appears ordinary to one person can convey the extraordinary to another? Why is a grain of sand merely a crumb of silicon to me, when to William Blake its crystalline reflections carried an image of the world? James thinks that's a product of our individual finitude. A creature with an infinite capacity for experience would find all of life tremendous, though, like the sun that blinds, mere mortals would find the vision overpowering. So we ration our wonders, the rationing being an unconscious process that arises from our make-up and past. The risk is that we ration ourselves too severely,

Figure 28
Mountains have long inspired a sense of the sublime and wonder, as in this painting, *A View of the Mountain Pass Called the Notch of the White Mountains* (1839) by Thomas Cole.

perhaps out of a fear that an experience of wonder might unsettle us. Then, though, life becomes nothing but a series of duties and necessities. But if we can cultivate the delight we find in that one thing, it can spill over into other parts of life and invigorate our sense of them too. On occasion, like when we fall in love, the world as a whole becomes lit up.

An epoch in our history

James captures the moment when that happens: 'This higher vision of an inner significance in what, until then, we had realized only in the dead external way, often comes over a person suddenly; and, when it does so, it makes an epoch in his history.' It springs upon us unawares, which is why the analogy of love-at-first-sight is so appropriate. Wonder is like that, even sometimes with the same kind of obsession.

It is the Romantics who have found the best words in modern times to express the force of it. The Romantics were not just interested in love. They were more interested in the unity of things, and how we can find the world to be a place that is enchanted. Their poems do not capture in any rational or logical way the sense in which Wordsworth, say, could ascribe 'a moral life' to 'every natural form, rock, fruit, or flower, | Even the loose stones that cover the highway.' But for his readers, who perhaps followed him across the high hills of the Lake District and had an intimation that this might be so, his words lend a form to their intuitions and allow them to stay with it. James writes:

'As Wordsworth walked, filled with his strange inner joy, responsive thus to the secret life of nature round about him, his rural neighbors, tightly and narrowly intent upon their own affairs, their crops and lambs and fences, must have thought him a very insignificant and foolish personage. It surely never occurred to any one of them to wonder what was going on inside of *him* or what it might be worth. And yet that inner life of his carried the burden of a significance that has fed the souls of others, and fills them to this day with inner joy.'

Wonder of wonders

There is a kind of wonder in wonder itself too. It stems from the fact that people find different things wonderful: that which evokes wonder in one person can look stupid or dull to another. Just why someone runs to embrace a tree, while another approaches its trunk to examine how to fell it, arises from an infinite store of memories, needs and intentions. James was quite sure that we should respect the things that cause others to wonder before we should judge them. He called it a 'blindness in human beings' that we find it so hard to respect the feelings of others. But it should be an affliction that is readily lifted. You only have to observe your dog, and the rapture it gains from a dry bone, damp hedges and lamp posts, to understand the universal feature of sentient beings is not found in *what* they find significant but in that they *find* significance in the world around them. Or think of the joy you find in reading yourself from your dog's point of view: 'To sit there like a senseless statue, when you might be taking him for a walk and throwing sticks for him to catch! What queer disease is this that comes over you every day. . .'

'Wonder. . . and not any expectation of advantage from its discoveries, is the first principle which prompts mankind to the study of Philosophy.'
Adam Smith

Everyday wonder

Williams is quite clear that wonder is a sense not only associated with the mystic or dreamer. You do not have to put to one side the practical pursuits of life in order to win a perception of life's meaning on the larger scale. Indeed, it may well be from within those practical pursuits that life's significance becomes clear.

Walt Whitman is his hero here, the poet who found the omnibus and ferry to be places of rapture equal to Wordsworth's mountain tops. It's just a question of attention and perspective. Hence, when Whitman was crossing from Brooklyn to Manhattan on the ferry, he remembered that the tides, which were rising and falling in the water beneath him, had being rising and falling for millennia before his crossing, and would continue to do so for millennia after the ferry had gone. The 'pouring in of the flood-tide' relativized the busyness of his existence, and in that he found the relief of wonder.

There is perhaps one capacity upon which this virtue rests more than any other. It is the capacity to take time. The individual who never has time to look or explore, but flits from one distraction to the next, will never know 'the preciousness of any hour', as James puts it. Walt Whitman's genius was to build opportunities for that preciousness into the everyday. He wrote a letter to a friend in which he describes the pattern of his day, focusing on the hours during which he travels from one part of the city to another. These are his moments of prayer, during which he is as awake to the world as a monk is while meditating. Whitman explains:

'You know it is a never ending amusement and study and recreation for me to ride a couple of hours on a pleasant afternoon on a Broadway stage in this way. You see everything as you pass, a sort of living, endless panorama – shops and splendid buildings and great windows.'

What does he see? How can the broad sidewalks show anything other than the crowd? James describes it as 'the eternal recurrence of the common order'. He continues: 'To be rapt with satisfied attention, like Whitman, to the mere spectacle of the world's presence, is one way, and the most fundamental way, of confessing one's sense of its unfathomable significance and importance.'

Taking time

It's not so much a question of sheer *quantity* of time, for wonder is not something that can be manufactured. Rather, it's to be able to experience a certain *quality* of time, though that in itself will take time to achieve. It's to be able to allow the humdrum distractions of the world to fall away. Or it's to put in the time as a kind of waiting for those moments when the sense of wonder breaks through. It can be frustrating. We live in a world in which we can light a room at the flick of a switch. Our tendency is to think that enlightenment should be possible more or less instantaneously too, and when it doesn't happen, to dismiss it. But James is optimistic, because moments of wonder are apparently a universal experience among humans. His research suggested that they are found in all parts of life, and not just when gazing at a beautiful vista or sitting inside a church.

A Step

Three secular miracles to assist with contemplation and wonder:

1 There's something, not nothing (call it existence).
2 We know we're existing (stones don't).
3 We can and often do find wonder in the fact.

30

Work – and becoming what you are

WE *spend the best days of the week, over the best years of our lives, doing it. So work is definitely something we need to consider. Moreover, while some people would say that they work to live, meaning that their real life does not take place in the confines of the office or factory, there is need for a warning. You become what you are. If you practise a certain way of life for roughly eight hours a day, then it'll forge you, shape you, form you.*

Hannah Arendt (1906–75)

Quick summary: One of the key philosophers of the twentieth century, Arendt studied with Heidegger before fleeing to the United States in 1941, having been detained as a Jew. As well as thinking about work, she wrote about love, particularly in the writings of Saint Augustine.

Key text: *The Human Condition* (1958) in which she developed some of her ideas about work, arguing that the pinnacle of human creativity was not thought but activity.

> 'For there is a perennial nobleness, and even sacredness, in Work.'
> Thomas Carlyle

A brief history

Work has long been regarded ambivalently. Hesiod, one of the poets of ancient Greece, wrote that work is good because it fills your barns with grain. Don't skip work, he argued, 'to gape at politicians and give ear to all the quarrels of the marketplace'. The Bible endorses work too, when it tells the

Figure 29 *Market Day in a Bohemian Mountain Town* (1833), etching by Carl Robert Croll. Work connects us to a great web of commerce and meaning.

story of God working on the mythical six days of creation – though he was wise enough to rest on the seventh.

But alongside that, work has also always been a heavy word. It's no coincidence that the French for it, *travail*, means 'woe' in English. Similarly, the Greek word for work, *ponos*, also means 'sorrow'. Words in other languages carry overtones of drudgery and adversity too – as Adam found, after the Fall, when he was condemned to wrestle his living from the soil. Little wonder the ancients tended to think that work was only to be engaged in when necessary. Best was to be an aristocrat, though the artisans who worked in workshops were admired by Plato and Aristotle for their artfulness and skill.

However, attitudes towards work took on a different dimension at the turn of modernity. During the sixteenth century, at the time of the Reformation, thinkers began to argue that work could be a vocation. It was not just monks and priests whose work was sanctified. Labourers and officials could regard their work as good too, and moreover seek satisfaction in doing it. Our expectations as to what work should deliver began to rise. As Martin Luther wrote: 'The works of monks and priests, be they never so holy and arduous, differ no whit in the sight of God from the works of the rustic toiling in the field or the woman going about her household tasks.' All jobs are to be valued. All jobs should deliver value.

The Norwegian philosopher Lars Svendsen, in his book entitled *Work*, summarizes it like this:

'We are extremely concerned with finding the *right* job. There should be a fit between the job and person. The idea is that a job can be right or wrong for you, depending on what sort of person you are. This was to some extent discussed already by Plato and Aristotle, but they considered it in rather different terms, as they wrote two thousand years before the emergence of modern individualism, and did not frame it in terms of the unique individual, but rather in terms of what class or general kind different people belong to. We frame it differently, in terms of every single individual having their own true vocation, which consists in becoming who they are meant to be as allegedly unique individuals.'

But in what way? How can these different tasks deliver meaning? What is it about the way we earn our crust that can be fulfilling? Hannah Arendt tried to answer these questions.

Labour and work

She noted that there is a difference between work and labour. It can be imagined by thinking about the difference between a monkey foraging for a banana and a human individual buying a banana.

The monkey does labour, in Arendt's schema. It's all quite simple for our evolutionary cousin. Hunger leads to search leads to food. Any old banana will do. That's really about it. Labour, then, is about little more than survival and reproduction. That's fine for monkeys. It would be dehumanizing for humans.

Which is why buying bananas is dramatically different for us. Before we've even set eyes on the yellow fruit, we'll have pondered the other choices available to us. Maybe you're fed up with bananas, for all that they're easy to eat. The struggle with peeling an orange would be worth it for the taste. (See how questions of choice, convenience and taste are already deeply implicated in the apparently simple work of buying a banana.)

Then you head for the supermarket, or fruit stall, and your choice there says much more about who you are again. Are you the kind of person that likes their fruit to look the right shape and colour? Perhaps you prefer to have it come pre-peeled for you too? Do you value price above all else? Do you prefer blackening bananas and so will head for the grocer who buys the cheaper stock from the wholesalers?

When you arrive at the retailers, you are immediately immersed in a great web of commerce that has led to the banana being ready for your purchase. There're folk who have sourced, grown, picked and shipped the banana. There are others who have selected, washed, priced and packaged the banana. There are others again who have considered where bananas should be placed in the shop, and assessed how many other banana seekers will visit to buy one. This is all part of what goes together to make up the phenomenon we call work. The work you do, seeking a banana, conducts you into a world of work and meaning, and connects you to all the other workers who are involved in this apparently simple act.

> *'There is nothing laudable in work for work's sake.'*
> John Stuart Mill

Stereotypes and personality types

To put it no more bluntly, if eating a banana makes you what you are, how much more so the career you choose, the vocation you pursue. The analysis explains why losing your job can be so devastating: you're losing a major constituent of your identity. It explains why we value some jobs more than others: more valuable jobs are those that appear more productive of meaningful and virtuous identities – teachers over managers, doctors over chemists, judges over lawyers.

Arendt wrote: 'Work and its product, the human artifice, bestow a measure of permanence and durability upon the futility of mortal life and the fleeting character of human time.' Work is that which transforms our natural, animal way of life, and which, through the pursuit of human needs and ends, makes the world a meaningful place. Any kind of work can, therefore, be said to be creative. The question is creative of what? Remember again that you become what you are. The bureaucrat, car salesman, politician and journalist speak of certain kinds of people in our minds, part stereotype for sure, but part personality type too. Who do *you* want to be?

Moral conflicts

Arendt's analysis also reveals why so many people can feel that what they do at work conflicts with who they feel they are. It's called alienation. You have to hang up your personal morality, along with your coat, at the door of the office. You treat people in the workplace in a way you'd never treat others at home. You exploit the world around you in your work in a way that you'd be embarrassed to admit if the details of the supply chains were laid out before you.

Then there's questions to ask about how your working life shapes your life as a whole. If it demands the best hours of the day from you, then how are you to save energy for the other things you'd like to do? This is the pressing question of work–life balance. John Locke, another philosopher who thought about work, argued that most human beings need to spend about three hours a day exercising their bodies in some way or other. He wasn't worried about waistlines. He was worried about psychological health.

Health and well-being aside, there's also the simple question of boredom. Adam Smith caught it well when he described what goes on in pin factories. 'One man draws out the wire, another straightens it, a third cuts it, a fourth points it, a fifth grinds it at the top for receiving the head: to make the head requires two or three distinct operations to put it on. . .' In the West, many have more fulfilling work – though only because we've exported the drudgery to places like China.

What's going on in all this is a confusion between the things that work produces and the workers who produce them. Good work is good for human beings. Much of what we call work is not.

Working lives

Nietzsche offers a final reflection here. He noted that with the development of the idea that work was a vocation, that the labourer's grind was as valuable as the priest's pastoralia, came something else. The boundaries between work and leisure become blurred. Every part of life comes to be shaped by values that originate in the workplace. 'Industrious races', he noted, 'find it very troublesome to endure leisure; it was a masterpiece of English instinct to make the Sabbath so holy and boring that the English begin unconsciously to lust for their work- and week-day.'

His challenge is, then, this. The values that pertain in the workplace have spilled over into our weekends and evenings, so that we rush around with the kids, sign up for an evening class, aggressively pursue some sport, devote hours to reading self-help books. It's as if everything must be judged by its efficiency and effectiveness. But perhaps we can push back a little, and judge at least some of what goes on at work by the standards we'd deploy elsewhere. Where do you find time for refreshment at work, for creativity, for others?

We're very aware of these tensions. We need to learn to cope with disappointments. Even the best work does not exist solely for your good alone, but for the good of the shareholders, customers and bosses. Progressive employers can work with these conflicts of interest to a degree. Some make substantial efforts to integrate the good of the company with the good of the employee. But perhaps Arendt offers a greater sense of hope that balance can be reached.

What her analysis allows us to see is that all sorts of details about the way we work matter. They all contribute to the person we become by working. It begins with how you *go* to work, continues with how you *behave* at work, deepens with the kind of satisfaction you *seek* from work – is the pay cheque all you want? And then there's the solidarity of working on things with others in a common task. It's why we make friends at work, and nothing contributes more to a happy life than friends.

Think of it, when you next buy a banana.

Credits

Internal images:
Figure 1 © Bjanka Kadic / Alamy
Figure 2 © The Art Archive / Musée du Louvre Paris
Figure 3 © Mary Evans Picture Library / Alamy
Figure 4 © Ludmiła Pilecka
Figure 5 © NASA
Figure 6 © The Art Archive / Hermitage Museum Saint Petersburg / Superstock
Figure 7 © The Art Archive / Kroller Muller Museum Otterlo / Superstock
Figure 8 © akg-images
Figure 9 © Photos 12 / Alamy
Figure 10 © The Granger Collection, NYC / TopFoto
Figure 11 © The Granger Collection, NYC / TopFoto
Figure 12 © Library of Congress
Figure 13 © The Art Archive / Alamy
Figure 14 © The Art Archive / Czartorysky Museum Cracow
Figure 15 MS. Ashmole 1511, fol. 46v. © The Bodleian Library, University of Oxford
Figure 16 © The Art Gallery Collection / Alamy
Figure 17 © INTERFOTO / Alamy
Figure 18 © ullsteinbild / TopFoto
Figure 19 © WILDLIFE GmbH / Alamy
Figure 20 © John Pratt/Keystone Features/Getty Images
Figure 21 © Tomas Abad / Alamy
Figure 22 © Dorling Kindersley / Getty Images
Figure 23 © The Art Archive / British Museum
Figure 24 © Library of Congress
Figure 25 © The Art Archive / Musée du Louvre Paris / Gianni Dagli Orti
Figure 26 © The Granger Collection, NYC / TopFoto
Figure 27 © www.wikipedia.org
Figure 28 © The Granger Collection, NYC / TopFoto
Figure 29 © Saxonia Gallery, Munich

Cover image:
© Ingram Publishing Limited

References

Aquinas, Thomas *Selected Philosophical Writings* (Oxford Paperbacks: 2008)
Arendt, Hannah *The Human Condition* (University of Chicago Press: 1958)
Aristotle, *The Nicomachean Ethics* (Penguin Classics: 2004)
Ballard, J.G. *Miracles of Life* (Fourth Estate: 2008)
Benedict (Saint) *The Rule of Saint Benedict* (Gracewing: 1990)
Buber, Martin *Between Man and Man* (Routledge Classics: 2002) and *I and Thou*
    (Continuum: 2004)
Coleridge, Samuel Taylor 'Aids to Reflection' in *Samuel Taylor Coleridge: The*
    Major Works (Oxford Paperbacks: 2008)
Collingwood, R.G. *The Principles of Art* (Clarendon Press: 1938)
Derrida, Jacques *On Cosmopolitanism and Forgiveness* (Routledge: 2001)
Dickinson, Emily *The Complete Poems* (Little, Brown & Company: 1988)
Erasmus, Desiderius *In Praise of Folly* (Penguin Classics: 2004)
Forster, E.M. *A Room With A View* (Penguin Classics: 2006)
Freud, Sigmund *Civilization and Its Discontents* (Hogarth Press: 1930)
Fromm, Erich *The Art of Loving* (Thorsons: 2010)
Heisenberg, Werner *Physics and Philosophy* (Penguin: 1990)
Houellebecq, Michel *Atomised* (Vintage: 2001)
Illich, Ivan and Cayley, David *The Rivers North of the Future* (House of Anansi
    Press: 2005)
McGilchrist, Iain *The Master and His Emissary* (Yale University Press: 2009)
James, William *The Varieties of Religious Experience* (Routledge Classics: 2008)
    and 'On a Certain Blindness in Human Beings' (Penguin Great Ideas: 2009)
Jung, Carl Gustav *Memories, Dreams, Reflections* (Pantheon Books: 1963)
Kandinsky, Wassily *Concerning the Spiritual in Art* (Dover: 1977)
Keynes, John Maynard *Economic Possibilities for Our Grandchildren* (1930,
    available online)
Kierkegaard, Søren *Fear and Trembling* (Penguin Classics: 2003)
Lao Tzu, *Tao Te Ching* (Wordsworth: 1997)
Leader, Darian *The New Black: Mourning, Melancholia and Depression* (Hamish
    Hamilton: 2008)
Lonergan, Eric *Money* (Acumen: 2009)
Lear, Jonathan *Freud* (Routledge: 2005)
Lovelock, James *The Vanishing Face of Gaia: A Final Warning* (Allen Lane: 2009)
MacIntyre, Alasdair *After Virtue* (University of Notre Dame Press: 1984)
Maitland, Sara *A Book of Silence* (Granta: 2008)

Marx, Karl *Economic and Philosophical Manuscripts of* 1844 (available online)

McCabe, Herbert *On Aquinas* (Burns & Oates: 2008) and *The Good Life* (Continuum: 2005)

Midgley, Mary *Beast and Man: The Roots of Human Nature* (Routledge: 1978) and *The Essential Mary Midgley* (Routledge: 2005)

Montaigne, Michel de *The Complete Essays* (Penguin Classics: 2004)

Murdoch, Iris *Metaphysics as a Guide to Morals* (Chatto & Windus: 1992) and *Existentialists and Mystics* (Chatto & Windus: 1997)

Nietzsche, Friedrich *Beyond Good and Evil* (Penguin Classics: 2003)

Nussbaum, Martha *The Fragility of Goodness* (Cambridge University Press: 1986) and *Love's Knowledge* (Oxford University Press: 1992)

Plato: *The Republic, Symposium, Phaedrus, Lysis* in *Plato: Complete Works* (Hackett Publishing: 1997)

Popper, Karl *Unended Quest* (Fontana: 1976)

Proust, Marcel *In Search of Lost Time: The Captive, The Fugitive* Volume 5 (Vintage: 1996)

Pullman, Philip *His Dark Materials Trilogy* (Scholastic: 2008) and *The Good Man Jesus and the Scoundrel Christ* (Canongate: 2010)

Russell, Bertrand *History of Western Philosophy* (Routledge Classics: 2004) , *Why I Am Not a Christian* (Routledge: 2004) and 'The Essence of Religion' in Greenspan, Louis and Andersson, Stefan *Russell on Religion* (Routledge: 1999)

Sandel, Michael J. *Justice* (Allen Lane: 2009)

Sartre, Jean-Paul *Being and Nothingness* (Routledge: 2003) and *Existentialism Is a Humanism* (Methuen: 2007)

Schopenhauer, Arthur *The World as Will and Representation, Volume II* (Dover: 1958) and *Essays and Aphorisms* (Penguin Classics: 1970)

Svendsen, Lars *Work* (Acumen: 2008)

Tolstoy, Leo *A Confession and Other Religious Writings* (Penguin Classics: 2005) and *Family Happiness and Other Stories* (Dover: 2005)

Tutu, Desmond 'My Credo' in Fadiman, Clifton *Living Philosophies* (Doubleday: 199)

Weil, Simone *An Anthology* (Penguin Classics: 2005) and *Gravity and Grace* (Routledge Classics: 2002)

Wilde, Oscar 'De Profundis' and 'The Soul of Man under Socialism' in *Complete Works of Oscar Wilde* (Collins Classics: 1994)

Index